100 Skill-Building Lessons Using 10 Favorite Books

A Teacher's Treasury of Irresistible Lessons
& Activities That Help Children Meet Learning
Goals in Reading, Writing, Math & More

BY SUSAN LUNSFORD

SCHOLASTIC
PROFESSIONAL BOOKS

NEW YORK • TORONTO • LONDON • AUCKLAND • SYDNEY
MEXICO CITY • NEW DELHI • HONG KONG • BUENOS AIRES

ACKNOWLEDGMENTS

 As Matthew hands me *The Bookshop Dog* for read-aloud, I smile and say, yet again, "This is one of my absolute favorite books." Someone is sure to remind me that "you always say that Mrs. Lunsford." It's true, I admit, I have hundreds of favorite books by favorite authors that I have identified over the years.

It is the enjoyment of sharing them with young children and seeing my excitement mirrored on their faces that makes my bookshelf of favorites continue to grow. I am thankful for the time I have had to share these wonderful books with children. Their enthusiasm for them has been the inspiration behind the lessons you are about to read.

I want to share ten of my favorite books and one hundred book-based activities so that you can enhance your own students' learning with ideas borrowed from the pages of favorite books. I would like to thank the following people who helped make this book a reality:

To Cindy Cowan
Thank you for your sharing your expertise, your classroom and thank you for your continued support of my ideas. You're a one-of-a-kind teacher and friend.

To Mrs. Cowan's second-grade class
Thank you for sharing your ideas and your enthusiasm for favorite books with me.

To the authors of my favorite books
Thank you for the endless opportunities you create for children and their teachers to love books together.

To my husband, Brad
Thank you, as always, for your constant support and encouragement.

To Ryan and Madison
Thank you for loving books with me.

Front cover and interior design by Kathy Massaro
Cover photograph by Bruce Cramer
Interior photographs on pages 8, 21, 36, 53, 68, 85, 98, 112, 131, and 147 by Bruce Cramer.
Interior illustrations by Maxie Chambliss

ISBN: 0-439-20579-4

Contents

Chapter 8   **Lucky to Have a Special Friend** 112

Chapter 9   **There Are Secrets All Around Us** 131

Chapter 10   **A Dog for a Week** 147

The Power of Children's Books

*Enjoying
a Favorite Book*

You know when a book has a powerful effect on children. They sit mesmerized, concentrating on the words as they are read, their expressions changing to anticipate the next event, to laugh at a character's actions, or to sympathize with a plight, their eyes scanning the illustrations for hints about what might happen next. Problems of the day, disagreements among friends, and the realities of everyday life vanish as readers enter the world created on the pages of an intriguing book. I relish such moments during read-aloud, anticipate the peaceful time each day, and regard it as the most valuable part of our daily routine. What better way to motivate beginning readers and writers, to help them view the world through another's eyes, and to bond with students than by sharing an irresistible book? And what better way to bring excitement to other areas of the school day than to relate activities to the characters, problems, and themes found in the pages of a favorite book?

Having used books successfully as springboards to writers' workshop and word power mini-lessons, I knew it was time to expand my literature-based lessons to include art, math, science, and social studies. One day as I was reading aloud *The Purple Coat* by Amy Hest, a new book-based lesson emerged. "Grampa's mouth is lined with pins," I read. "He measures her arms, from shoulders to fingertips. He measures her legs from the heel up, and her waist, and across the top of her chest. When there is nothing left to measure, he kisses the tip of her nose." As I held the book for students to see, Ben stretched his arms like Gabby and said, "I bet it's hard to stand so still for so long—especially if it tickles!" "Maybe we should give it a try," I said, as it occurred to me that Gabby's purple coat would add a little excitement to our introduction to measurement the next day.

By the end of that week, *The Purple Coat* had inspired ten lessons. The success of these lessons encouraged me to develop similar lessons using other books. Once again, I discovered that good books make some of the most ordinary learning goals more exciting for students and myself. Throughout the course of the school year, Kevin Henkes' *Chrysanthemum* and her friends introduced quotation marks; Rosemary Wells' *Yoko* helped students practice estimating and counting, while *Arthur's Teacher Trouble* gave reason to practice careful spelling techniques and Judith Viorst's *Alexander and the Terrible, Horrible, No Good, Very Bad Day* taught students the importance of silent 'e'.

The Art Lesson by Tomie dePaola provided an opportunity for writing with analogies while Lois Ehlert's *Top Cat* assisted with using context clues and Cynthia Rylant's *The Bookshop Dog* showed how to outline a story. A couple of Steven Kellogg's *Best Friends* helped to solve problems in written stories while Eve Bunting's *Night Tree* inspired writing rich in sensory detail. These favorites received a great deal of mileage in our classroom and provided inspiration for this book.

100 Skill-Building Lessons Using 10 Favorite Books is all about using the power of children's books to help students meet learning goals across the curriculum. Each chapter presents a mini-lesson from my classroom based on one of ten featured books. An independent practice or follow-up lesson is described along with eight more book-based activities for use on other days. Read each of the books with your students just for the pleasure and bonding time they will afford you. Then use the mini-lessons to motivate students and allow them to relate learning to the characters, events, and words found in the pages of these wonderful stories.

Admittedly, the most difficult part of writing this book was narrowing my endless list of favorites to just ten books. The ones I have chosen all relate to something in my own life, which makes my time spent sharing them and depicting them as favorites genuine. These stories about dogs and cats, family traditions, problems at school and among friends, have inspired some of my most successful lessons. The books are not ranked in any order. Instead, they are listed in the order that I share them each new school year.

Use the ideas in this book to motivate your students, and adapt them to suit your needs and teaching style. Most important, use the ideas as inspiration for other lessons based on your own favorite books. Let your students' enthusiasm for certain works of literature spark ideas of your own and help you build a collection of favorite books and book-based lessons that will add a new twist to otherwise ordinary lessons. Let the power of children's books help your students meet with success across the curriculum, beginning with just ten books to teach one hundred lessons.

Chapter One

School Is No Place for Me!

LESSONS 1 TO 10

Chrysanthemum
by Kevin Henkes

Mini-Lessons Across the Curriculum

Chrysanthemum Said

GOAL *Exploring Quotation Marks*

> ❝**C**hrysanthemum loved the way her name looked when it was written with ink on an envelope. She loved the way it looked when it was written with icing on her birthday cake. And she loved the way it looked when she wrote it herself with her fat orange crayon. Chrysanthemum, Chrysanthemum, Chrysanthemum. Chrysanthemum thought her name was absolutely perfect. And then she started school...❞
>
> ~*Chrysanthemum* by Kevin Henkes, pp. 7–8.

 In telling Chrysanthemum's story, Kevin Henkes captures the words of young children and their adults in realistic dialogue. From Mrs. Chud's weary response of "Thank you for sharing that with us, Victoria, now put your head down" to Chrysanthemum's bold statement that "school is no place for me," students and teachers alike can relate to the sentiments expressed in characters' authentic voices. Bringing the conversations between Chrysanthemum and her classmates and family to a mini-lesson on quotation marks puts a clever twist on the typical introduction of this topic. In the lesson that follows, beginning readers can use Chrysanthemum's words to practice reading dialogue with expressive voices while learning about the proper placement of quotation marks using "talking macaroni marks."

Since elbow macaroni is shaped exactly like quotation marks, I buy a box and cover the label with a piece of paper that reads "Talking Macaroni Marks" (see the tip on page 10). I copy the "talking macaroni sentences" (see page 11) from *Chrysanthemum* on chart paper, omitting the quotation marks, and gather my students around me. What used to be a difficult concept for beginning readers and writers now becomes a memorable lesson filled with giggles and greater understanding—all with the help of *Chrysanthemum* and a box of elbow macaroni. The lesson usually goes something like this:

Collin: What's in the box?

Mrs. L.: Talking macaroni marks. It says so on the label.

Lauren: Talking macaroni marks?

Mrs. L.: That's what's in the box. It seems some of the most important punctuation marks are missing from these sentences. Without these special marks, it will be difficult to read the sentences with expression and good understanding. So I brought some talking marks with me.

Sam: What do they look like?

Mrs. L.: I'll show you. These are talking marks [I copy a set of quotation marks on the board]. These are talking macaroni marks [I hold up two pieces of elbow macaroni].

Stephanie: The macaroni looks just like the talking marks. I bet that's why you call them talking macaroni marks.

Mrs. L.: That's right! You've probably seen authors use curved lines like these around words in stories to show that a character is saying certain words. When Kevin Henkes wrote *Chrysanthemum*, he used marks like this to show when Chrysanthemum and her family and classmates were talking.

Molly: I've never heard of talking marks.

Mrs. L.: The fancy name for these marks is *quotation marks*. For now, why don't we call these quotation marks talking marks?

Jack: Talking marks is easier to remember.

Mrs. L.: I agree, and quotation marks show that someone is talking.

Ben: And I bet we're going to stick the macaroni marks on the chart when we know someone is talking.

Mrs. L.: Right again! I thought this might be more fun than just using a pencil and drawing the talking marks. We'll use sticky tack to put the talking macaroni marks around the words spoken by a character in these sentences from *Chrysanthemum*. Let's read the first sentence together:

Class: *She's perfect, said her mother.*

Mrs. L.: Tell me who is talking in this sentence.

Mary: Chrysanthemum's mom.

Mrs. L.: Right. And what words does Chrysanthemum's mother say?

Hannah: She says, *she's perfect.*

Mrs. L.: Great. Let's put some talking macaroni marks around the words *she's perfect*. Every new time a character says something, we'll need four pieces of macaroni. Two marks are used to show where she begins talking, and two marks are used to show where she stops talking. I'll put two talking marks on each side of the words *she's perfect*.

Ben: Talking marks are easy!

Mrs. L.: That's because you are good thinkers. Notice how the talking marks where mother begins talking point toward the word *she's*. The ones where she stops talking point toward the word *perfect*.

Stephanie: The talking marks sort of hold on to the words.

Alex: And it takes two talking marks to hold on to each side of the words she says.

Mrs. L.: Good thinking! Let's try the next sentence:

Class: *Hooray! said Chrysanthemum. School!*

Mrs. L.: Tell me which words Chrysanthemum is saying.

Courtney: *Hooray.*

Ben: Chrysanthemum also said the word *school.*

Mrs. L.: You're right. *Hooray* and *school* are the words Chrysanthemum said. I'll place a pair of talking marks in front of the word *hooray.*

Alex: Put the other talking marks after the word *school.* Chrysanthemum said that word, too.

Mrs. L.: Yes, she did.

Tori: But she didn't say *said.* She only said *hooray.* The *said Chrysanthemum* part just tells you who is talking.

Mrs. L.: More good thinking! Since Kevin Henkes interrupted Chrysanthemum's words to remind us of who was talking, *hooray* has to be held by one set of talking marks. Then the word *school* is held by another set of talking marks.

Matthew: Then you'll need eight macaroni marks for that sentence.

Mrs. L.: Good counting.

Talking Macaroni Sentences

She's perfect, said her mother.

Hooray! said Chrysanthemum. School!

School is no place for me, said Chrysanthemum. My name is too long. It scarcely fits on my name tag. And I'm named after a flower!

If I had a name like yours, I'd change it, Victoria said as the students lined up to go home.

What's so humorous? asked Mrs. Twinkle.

Chrysanthemum's a daisy! Chrysanthemum's a daisy! Jo, Rita, and Victoria chanted, thinking it was wildly funny.

During nap time Victoria raised her hand and said, A chrysanthemum is a flower. It lives in a garden with worms and other dirty things.

I demonstrate the proper placement of talking marks in this sentence: *"Hooray!" said Chrysanthemum. "School!"*

Anna: Why don't you just put two talking marks at the beginning of the sentence and two more talking marks at the end when she is finished talking?

Mrs. L.: You mean like this?

I remove the talking marks after the word hooray and before the word school: *"Hooray! said Chrysanthemum. School!"*

Madison: Then the words *said Chrysanthemum* would be talking words, too, and they aren't.

Mrs. L.: Excellent thinking. Matthew was right —I need eight talking macaroni marks for this sentence, not just four. Now let's read the sentence using a talking voice for those words inside of the talking marks:

Class: *"Hooray!" said Chrysanthemum. "School!"*

Mrs. L.: Great job! Let's try another sentence that needs eight talking marks because Kevin Henkes wanted to give us a reminder of who was saying this sentence. [I point and the class reads:]

Class: *School is no place for me, said Chrysanthemum. My name is too long. It scarcely fits on my name tag. And I'm named after a flower!*

Mrs. L.: Chrysanthemum doesn't talk about how excited she is about school in this sentence, does she? What does Chrysanthemum say?

David: She said *school is no place for me.*

Mrs. L.: Let's put talking marks around those words. Does she say anything else?

Elizabeth: She says her name is too long.

Mrs. L.: Anything else?

David: *It scarcely fits on my name tag.*

Lauren: *And I'm named after a flower.*

Mrs. L.: Good reading.

Lauren: Chrysanthemum said a lot of things.

Mrs. L.: You're right. We can use one set of talking marks around all the words that she says—as long as these words are not interrupted by a reminder of who is talking.

Eric: *School is no place for me* is the first thing Chrysanthemum says.

Emma: Don't put talking marks around *Chrysanthemum said.*

Mrs. L.: O.K. The next time Chrysanthemum starts talking, she says three whole sentences before she stops. Please read these sentences with me:

Class: *My name is too long. It scarcely fits on my name tag. And I'm named after a flower!*

Mrs. L.: We can put one set of talking marks around all of these words— a pair of talking marks in front of the word *my* and a pair after the word *flower.* Let's read these sentences with the talking marks:

Class:	*"School is no place for me," said Chrysanthemum. "My name is too long. It scarcely fits on my name tag. And I'm named after a flower!"*
Mrs. L.:	I like the way you read the words inside the talking marks with expression.
Sam:	I used a special voice when Chrysanthemum was talking.
Mrs. L.:	Now that you know about talking marks, it should be easier to read with expression. Talking marks are a reminder to make your voice sound like a particular character is talking. Please read the next sentence with me:
Class:	*If I had a name like yours, I'd change it, Victoria said as the students lined up to go home.*
Hannah:	I don't think Victoria was very nice so I read the words in a kind of bratty voice.
Mrs. L.:	Good thinking. Which of the words in this sentence did you read as if Victoria was saying them?
Tori:	*If I had a name like yours, I'd change it.*
Mrs. L.:	Let's put the talking marks around these words. There are quite a few words left in this sentence.
Jack:	But nobody says them. Kevin Henkes just added some extra words.
Madison:	I like these extra words. They tell that Victoria said the words as the students lined up to go home and I can picture it.
Matthew:	That means the kids picked on poor Chrysanthemum the whole day!
Molly:	But you don't need to use any talking marks.
Mrs. L.:	Great. The word *said* is just one word that should give you a hint that you are going to have to use talking marks. As we read the next sentence, look for another word that can be used to show someone is speaking.

    We read the rest of the sentences on the chart, adding quotation marks and discussing where to put them. I ask students to copy the last sentence on paper and glue talking macaroni marks around the words that show someone is talking.

Independent Practice

Talking Macaroni Marks:
Practicing Quotation Marks

With a sheet of paper, pencil, glue, and four pieces of macaroni, the students work independently to punctuate the following sentence with talking marks: *During naptime, Victoria raised her hand and said, "A Chrysanthemum is a flower. It lives in a garden with worms and other dirty things."*

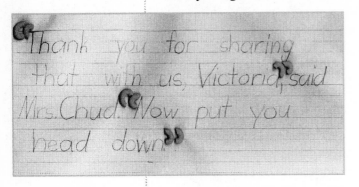

We discuss the proper placement of the talking macaroni marks before I collect the sheet for safe keeping. The next morning as the students arrive, I have them copy Mrs. Chud's response to Victoria, adding eight macaroni pieces to the practice sheet as needed.

With practice, the students become more conscious of those words that are spoken by a particular character. When reading aloud, talking marks become red flags for speaking in a character's voice. In written work, editing for talking marks is a less confusing task thanks to the help we received from Chrysanthemum and her friends. As we continue to discuss conversations between characters in the many other books we read, students' awareness of quotation marks continues to grow. Those mysterious marks once overlooked by the beginning reader's eye now add new meaning to a story.

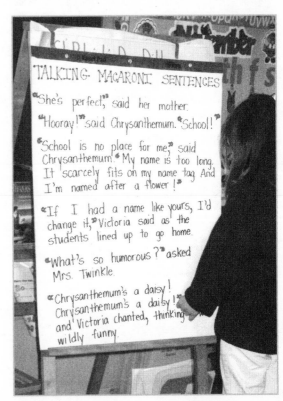

Talking Macaroni Sentences ▶

8 More Book-Based Lessons

Learning the Golden Rule: Role-Playing Difficult Situations

Have your students put themselves in Chrysanthemum's shoes during a little role-playing fun. Create scenes involving characters from *Chrysanthemum,* such as those listed below, and copy onto separate index cards (one scene per card). After dividing the class into small groups of actors, distribute one card to each group. Have each group plan a short skit to perform for classmates. Each skit should demonstrate the importance of treating others the way we wish to be treated. Following each skit, talk about other ways Chrysanthemum might face the challenges of her classmates' ridicule by setting an example of kindness toward others.

▲ *Role-Playing with Chrysanthemum & Friends*

Role-Playing Scenarios from Chrysanthemum

At lunchtime, Victoria tells Chrysanthemum that people named after flowers are not allowed to sit at her table. "Maybe you should go eat lunch with the worms that live in the dirt like flowers," Victoria says.

The day after Jo, Rita and Victoria call Chrysanthemum names, they want to play with the fancy jewelry-making kit that Chrysanthemum has brought to school. "My Aunt Daisy gave it to me for my birthday," Chrysanthemum says as she tries to decide what to do.

At recess, Victoria trips over a jump rope and tears her new dress. Jo and Rita laugh at her. In tears, Victoria looks to Chrysanthemum for help. "Jo and Rita are being so mean to me," Victoria complains.

Words We Know: Practicing "Book Spelling"

▲ *Our Word Wall*

Use the illustration on page 16 of *Chrysanthemum* to reinforce careful spelling with your beginning writers. Label a large sheet of black butcher-block paper with the title "Words We Know." Invite students to write words they know with book spelling on this "chalkboard" using white chalk—just like Chrysanthemum's class! As one volunteer writes a book-spelled word on the chart, the rest of the class copies the word onto individual lap boards.

Using chart paper allows your "word wall" to be conveniently moved to a more permanent place when complete. Students now have a handy reference for future book-spelling attempts. Periodically, take a few minutes to add other words that have become committed to memory by your class.

Name Your Space: Creating Name Tags for Student Work

Chrysanthemum loved the way her name looked when it was written in ink, with icing, and with her fat orange crayon. In this art activity, your students can explore ways they love their names to look while creating unique name labels for displayed work. Cut one 6 by 12 inch strip of oak tag for each student (longer names may require a longer strip); then place a scrap box of materials, letter stencils, and other art supplies (such as sequins, felt, pipe cleaners, tissue paper scraps, etc.) in one central location.

Students begin by writing their names using the letter stencils or their own block lettering on a strip of oak tag. Next, students decorate each letter in a different way with markers or crayons—polka-dots, stripes, and stars are a few common enhancements. Accents of yarn, glitter, sequins, or other items can be added to make the name tags special.

▲ *A Student Name Tag*

Hugs, Kisses, & Parcheesi: Exploring Plural Endings

Chrysanthemum always felt better after an evening filled with hugs, kisses, and Parcheesi. What is it that makes students cheer up when they're feeling down? Chocolates, smiles, or walks in the park? Use Chrysanthemum's perfect evening of hugs, kisses, and Parcheesi as a springboard for exploring plural endings. As students discuss their favorite things, list each idea in its plural form on a chart labeled "Hugs, Kisses, Parcheesi, & Other Happy Things." After gathering a sufficient list of items, highlight each *-s* or *-es* ending with a yellow marker. Discuss any special words (like *puppies*) in which "*y* changes to *i* before adding *-es*." This activity not only arms students with happy thoughts to get them through difficult days, but also offers assistance when writing words that mean more than one.

Hugs, Kisses, Parcheesi, & Other Happy Things

smiling faces	chocolates	cookies	friends
walks in the park	moms	flowers	dads
books	teddy bears	kittens	pictures
puppies	good memories	games	pizzas
snuggles	good cries		

My Name Is...: Discovering Name Origins

Chrysanthemum's parents wanted her name to be "everything she is," to be "absolutely perfect." Have your students do a little homework to find out how they came to be given their particular names. Were they named after a grandfather? A parent? Did an older sibling get the final vote? Did deciding on a name take months of pondering or was it figured out in a snap? If there is a namesake, what information can be given about this person?

Have students copy the short reminder note at right to prompt them to inquire about the origin of their names. Invite students to write a story about their name based on research done at home. Spend a few moments each day asking for volunteers to share their name discoveries.

Homework

Jot down a few sentences about how I came to be named Matthew.

The Name Game:
Sorting Words by Attributes

This activity helps students sharpen their observational and classifying skills by sorting names of classmates by common attributes. Before the lesson, write students' first names on oak tag strips—or use the name tags created in "Name Your Space," above. Select a few names according to a particular attribute and place them on the chalk ledge. The students must guess what the selected names have in common. For example, I place Madison, Matthew, Molly, and Mary's name on the chalk ledge. Students quickly notice that these are all the names beginning with the letter *M.* Next I place the names *Mary* and *Molly* on the chalk ledge with the name *Courtney* for students to determine that these names end in *y.* For names with four letters, I group *Jack, Eric, Alex, Tori, Anna,* and *Mary* together.

After testing your students observational skills with these more obvious attributes, try a few more challenging ones: Matthew, Hannah, Collin, Molly, and Anna all have double consonants while Eric, Elizabeth, Alex, and Anna are all names that begin with vowels. Anna, Ben, Courtney, David, and Eric are arranged in alphabetical order, while Mary, Sam, Sarah, Lauren, Hannah, David, Samantha, Matthew, Jack, and Madison all have the letter *A* as a second letter. There is an endless number of ways to classify the names of students. As time allows, invite students to select names with a common attribute for classmates to figure out. End each round by asking if there are any other names that should be added to the group.

Playing the Name Game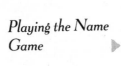

Name the Syllables:
Identifying Syllables in Words

Like "The Name Game" (above), "Name the Syllables" helps students explore similarities and differences in names of class members, this time according to the number of beats per name. Chrysanthemum's name has four syllables, just like Victoria's; Rita's name has two beats and Jo's has only one. With these characters' names listed on the board, I give each student a name tag (recycled from "The Name Game") and we gather to identify the number of beats or syllables in our names. We clap the names *A-lex-an-der* and *E-liz-a-beth* and then add these name tags to the list of names with four beats just like Chry-san-the-mum and Vic-tor-i-a. Sam, Ben, and Jack add their names to the one-beat names. We discover that two-beat names are the most common in our class, while three-beat names tie with those having one syllable. We add other character names and special guests as we meet them. As our list grows, so does our awareness of syllables. On another day, we draw lines to show where the syllables break apart and discover a new tactic for attacking unknown words "one beat at a time."

One-Syllable Names	Two-Syllable Names	Three-Syllable Names	Four-Syllable Names
Jo	Rita	Stephanie	Chrysanthemum
Sam	Matthew	Madison	Victoria
Ben	Eric	Samantha	Alexander
Jack	David		Elizabeth
	Hannah		
	Lauren		
	Tyler		
	Collin		
	Molly		
	Sarah		
	Tori		
	Courtney		
	Anna		
	Mary		

Chrysanthemums, Daisies, & Lilies: Growing Flowers from Seeds

Let *Chrysanthemum* inspire students to give indoor flower gardening a try. After brainstorming a list of flowers and voting on a few kinds to grow, make a list of other materials needed for planting. Gather these materials before the next science lesson. Using paper cups, a bag of planting soil, and plastic spoons, students select a few flower seeds to plant. Students can choose whether they wish to place one or more kinds of seeds in their cups. After filling the cups half-full of dirt, students sprinkle in a few seeds before adding a top layer of soil. After an initial watering, the plants are placed on a windowsill.

Each morning, remind students to check their flowers and water as needed. Once a week, take the first five minutes of science time to record the growth of plants in individual Flower Journals. In a short time, students have some chrysanthemums, lilies, and daisies ready to take home for transplanting.

A Flower Journal Entry
▼

Dec 19, 2000

Today I planted flower seeds. I hope they will grow into daisies soon.

More Books by Kevin Henkes

A Weekend with Wendell (Greenwillow, 1986)

Baily Goes Camping (Greenwillow, 1997)

Chester's Way (William Morrow & Company, 1988)

Julius, the Baby of the World (Greenwillow, 1990)

Lily's Purple Plastic Purse (Greenwillow, 1996)

Owen (Greenwillow, 1993)

Sheila Rae, the Brave (Greenwillow, 1987)

Wemborly Worried (Greenwillow, 2000)

Chapter Two

What's Funny About Purple?

LESSONS 11 TO 20

The Purple Coat
by Amy Hest

Mini-Lessons Across the Curriculum

Language Arts

Purple, Red, and Pumpkin Leaves	*Writing descriptive story starters*
Fringed Moccasins and Wooly Arms	*Using describing words*
Grampa, Gabrielle, and Pastrami	*Studying consonant blends*
Character Report Cards	*Evaluating character traits*

Math & Science

Measuring Me	*Exploring length using non-standard units of measurement*
Measuring for New Coats	*Practicing with nonstandard units of measurement*
More Measuring Fun	*Making tape measures*

Community

Purple on One Side, Navy on the Other	*Resolving conflicts through compromise*
Map of the City	*Designing a community*

Art

The Perfect Coat	*Designing original creations*

Measuring Me

GOAL *Exploring Length Using Non-Standard Units of Measurement*

THE PURPLE COAT

AMY HEST
pictures by
AMY SCHWARTZ

> ❝ Gabby moves toward the neat rows of fabric on the wall opposite. She drags red-painted fingertips, slowly, across the rainbow of colors stacked in open shelves way up to the ceiling and down to the polished wood floor. "Hello Purple," she whispers, pausing on the prettiest shade of all. ❞
>
> ~ *The Purple Coat* by Amy Hest, pp. 14–15.

The Purple Coat takes readers to Gabby's grandfather's city tailor shop for her annual new coat fitting. This year, even though Gabby likes the fact that the deli sandwiches and Grampa's green sweater are the same, she wants the color of her coat to be different because "once in a while it's good to try something new." After reading aloud and discussing Amy Hest's many examples of descriptive language, I bring this book to a math lesson for a real-life application of measurement. Our classroom becomes "Room 4's Tailor Shop," where partners work together to fit each other for new purple, fuchsia, tangerine, and a few polka-dotted coats.

Since two inches on a ruler is not as clear to see as two objects placed side-by-side, the process of measuring can be made more tangible for young children by using non-standard units found in the classroom. Aside from being more hands-on, lining up plastic teddy bears, Unifix cubes, and Learning Links next to objects makes measuring more fun and helps young mathematicians practice proper measuring techniques. If your students' goal is measuring in standard units, collect tape measures like those used by tailors to give students practice measuring in centimeters or inches.

To prepare for this lesson, I gather manipulatives from our classroom and make a copy of the "Measuring Me" recording sheet found on page 34 for each child. Then I don my emerald coat, uncuff the sleeves to make them appear too long, and meet the students on the carpet for a lesson on Measuring Me.

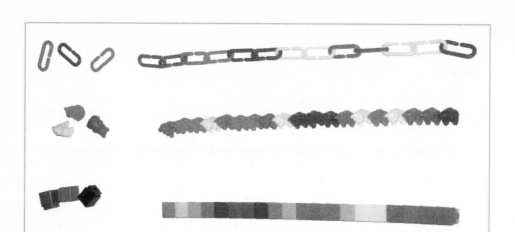

▲ *Unifix Cubes, Teddy Bear Counters, and Learning Links*

Teaching Tip

For the demonstration below, you may wish to borrow a friend's coat that is either too big or too small. In years past, I've worn my husband's coat to help make a greater impression of an ill-fitting garment. Or you might try bringing a coat that is either too big or too small for one of your students to model as you demonstrate how to make appropriate measurements.

Any items found in your classroom can be used for measuring in non-standard units. The items we use in the following mini-lesson are pictured above.

Tyler: Why are you wearing your coat for math time, Mrs. L.?

David: Your sleeves are too long.

Mrs. L.: I thought if I wore my coat for our math lesson, you might be able to help me figure out the problem with my coat sleeves. Just like Grampa and Gabby in *The Purple Coat*, I need your help with a fitting for my emerald green coat. I'm not sure if I ordered the right size from the catalog. Listen as I read the page where Gabrielle is being fitted for her purple coat. Tell me what the fittings have to do with math.

> "I hate the fittings," she complains a few minutes later. Grampa's mouth is lined with pins. He measures her arms, from shoulders to fingertips. He measures her legs from the heel up, and her waist, and across the top of her chest. When there is nothing left to measure, he kisses the tip of her nose.

Stephanie: We need to measure your arms. We're going to be measuring.

Mrs. L.: Of course! Uh, oh. I don't have a tape measure. But I do have lots of Unifix cubes. We could put a whole line of them together just like a ruler.

Tori: Without the numbers.

Mrs. L.: Great idea. I'll take off my coat.

Matthew: We should measure your arm from your shoulder to your hand.

David: Grampa measured from Gabby's shoulder to her fingertips.

Mrs. L.: You're right. I'm not growing like Gabby so there doesn't have to be room for me to grow in my coat. I'll take off my coat so you can measure the length of my arm. Estimate how many Unifix cubes long you think my arm is from shoulder to wrist.

Sam: I say 20.

Courtney: No 30.

Ben: I say more like 42.

Hannah:	45.
Alex:	50.
Mrs. L.:	Any other ideas?
Jack:	40.
Mrs. L.:	Great estimating. Molly, would you please help me measure my arm?
Molly:	Sure.

I purposely do not line the end of the Unifix cubes up with the end of my shoulder.

Molly:	No, you have to put the end of the Unifix cubes right at the end of your shoulder.
Mrs. L.:	Tell me why it is so important to line my Unifix ruler up exactly with the end of my shoulder.
Molly:	If you don't, your measurement won't be accurate—your sleeve could be too long or too short.
Mrs. L.:	Looks like my arm is about 30 cubes.
Courtney:	That was my estimate! I got it right.
Mrs. L.:	That is excellent estimating, Courtney.
Sam:	You should measure your coat sleeve now to see how much too long it is.
Mrs. L.:	Great idea. Sam, please help me do that.
Anna:	Put the Unifix ruler right on the end of the shoulder of the coat.
Mary:	Right at the seam. Measure to the end of your sleeve. It looks like it's 40.
Madison:	That's 10 Unifix cubes too long.
Eric:	The sleeves should be 10 Unifix cubes shorter.
Mrs. L.:	That looks about right to me. Just for fun, let's try measuring my arm using Teddy Bear Counters.
Samantha:	They don't snap together. But you could lie down flat and we'll place the Teddy Bears on the floor along your arm.
Mrs. L.:	Great idea! Do you think my arm will measure more Teddy Bears than Unifix cubes, less, or about the same?
Samantha:	The Teddy Bears are bigger than the cubes, so I know it will take fewer Teddy Bears to measure your arm.
Tori:	I think it depends on whether you are going to stand the bears up side by side or lay them down head to toe.
Molly:	They will sit up better side-by-side.
Matthew:	Or, you could line the Teddy Bears up beside the 30 Unifix cubes.
Mrs. L.:	Good thinking! Any estimates of how long my arm will be in Teddy Bears?
Matthew:	25.
Tyler:	15—the Teddy Bears look bigger than the Unifix cubes.
David:	I say 20.
Stephanie:	Me, too.

Mrs. L.:	Good estimating. Ben, would you help me measure my arm, please? I'll lie down and you can put the Teddy Bears side-by-side along my arm. While we're doing this measuring, Collin, would you line Teddy Bears up beside the 30 Unifix cubes so we can double-check our results?
Ben:	Your arm is 28 Teddy Bears long.
Collin:	And it takes 28 Teddy Bears to line up with 30 Unifix Cubes.
Samantha:	We were right. It takes fewer Teddy Bears than Unifix Cubes.
Eric:	Can we measure your arm in learning links? We can link them together and pull them tight. They'll be almost like a ruler.
Mrs. L.:	Why don't you snap a few together, Eric. How do you think the learning links will compare to the Unifix cubes and the Teddy bears when measuring? Will it take more or less links than Unifix Cubes or Teddy Bear Counters?
Alex:	Well, they are bigger than the cubes and the bears. So it will take less learning links.
Mrs. L.:	Great. Let's make some estimates before we measure.
Hannah:	12.
Emma:	15.
Lauren:	25.
Elizabeth:	22.
Jack:	14.
Mrs. L.:	You are great estimators. Now let's see how close our estimates are to the real measurement.

When we get to my wrist, the link doesn't line up exactly with my wrist but goes past my wrist to the middle of my hand.

Matthew:	That means your hand is 17 and a half links long.
Jack:	No, I think it's closer to 18 links.
Molly:	If you were using a real ruler, it would be on one of the lines in between the big numbers. I guess that's why those little lines are on rulers. Grampa has to be a very good measurer to be a tailor!
Tori:	Or Gabby's coat wouldn't fit.
Mrs. L.:	You're right. I see how important it is to measure carefully. I should have measured more carefully before I ordered my emerald green coat. It is important to line up the end of the ruler with the end of the item being measured. It's also important to estimate before measuring so that you have an idea of what your measurement should be.
Sam:	You also need to be a good counter and know your numbers.

Independent Practice

Measuring for New Coats: Practicing with Non-Standard Units of Measurement

Mrs. L.: Today, you will have a chance to be fitted for your own purple coat.

Lauren: Or tangerine?

Mrs. L.: Sure! As Grampa told Gabby, "once in a while, it's good to try something new." So, today, we're going to work at Room 4's City Tailor Shop, measuring each other for our own perfect coats. I have a recording sheet to help you remember the measurements that you need to make. You and a measuring partner can choose whatever item you want for measuring. Just remember, the items you measure with must be the same—you couldn't use 12 balls of different sizes.

Madison: Or different kinds of pattern blocks.

Mrs. L.: Right. Remember to practice lining up the end of your measuring "tape" with the item being measured.

Matthew: Are we estimating?

Mrs. L.: Yes. On the recording sheet there is a space for you to make estimates before measuring. There is also a line for the actual measurements.

After the lesson, we meet to discuss the problem I would have if I actually went to a tailor and said I needed my sleeves to be 14 Unifix Cubes long. We discuss why tailors need to use standard measuring devices such as tape measures so that everyone is speaking the same "measuring language." On another day, we get some practice measuring in inches and centimeters, using the same recording sheet and a tape measure.

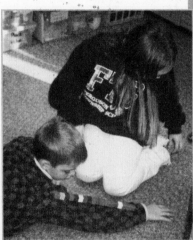

Measuring One Another for New Coats

A Completed Recording Sheet ▷

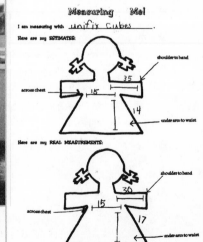

8 More Book-Based Lessons

More Measuring Fun:
Making Tape Measures

Students enjoy making their own paper tape measures or rulers in this lesson, which helps students move from concrete to picture representation of measurement. Cut one

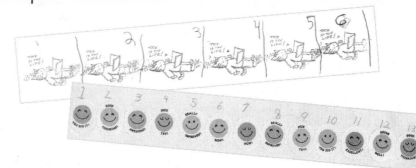

twelve-inch section of adding machine paper or oak tag for each student. Students select an object such as a block for tracing or place rubber stamps or stickers one beside the other on the paper tape measure. Then they add numbers above or below each picture. After the measuring tapes are completed, students measure items around the classroom and compare with measurements of classmates using a different "standard" for measurement.

If time allows, have students use the reverse side of their paper ruler to record actual inches and/or centimeters with markings from an actual ruler. This two-in-one ruler now allows students to compare items measured using standard and non-standard units.

▲ *Two Student-Made Rulers*

Measuring with Our Rulers

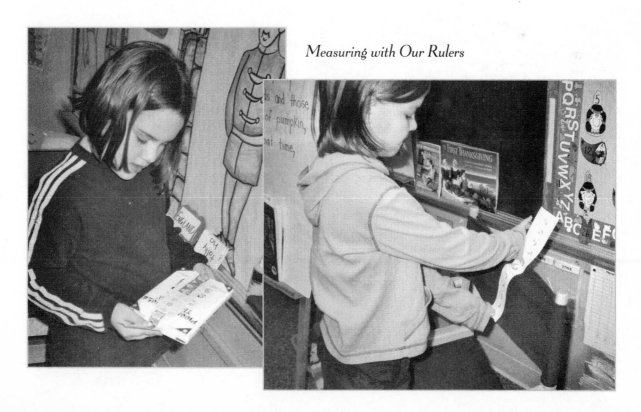

Purple, Red, and Pumpkin Leaves: Writing Descriptive Story Starters

Use the teamwork of author Amy Hest and illustrator Amy Schwartz to help your fledgling writers improve the beginnings of their stories. On the first page of *The Purple Coat*, Amy Hest writes: "Every fall, when the leaves start melting into pretty purples and reds and those bright golden shades of pumpkin, Mama says, 'Coat time, Gabrielle!'"

In illustrating the first page of *The Purple Coat*, Amy Schwartz took hints from the writers' words. She drew a rake leaning against a tree with purple- and pumpkin-colored leaves falling from its branches; Mama, holding a mug of steaming coffee or tea stands on the front porch with Gabby. With one sock drooping at her ankle, Gabby buttons her sweater against the chilly autumn air. This author and illustrator complement each other's work nicely.

Invite students to choose one of their own stories and illustrate its opening scene in great detail. Then encourage them to revise their beginning sentence to include some of the details from their illustrations. Remind them how the extra words Amy Hest added to her beginning sentence and the many illustrating details Amy Schwartz used make *The Purple Coat* a favorite book. Ask students to compare both versions of their story's beginning and discuss how the illustrations and details change it.

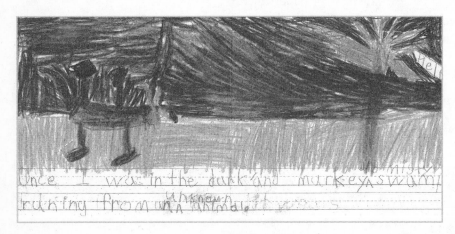

Once I was in the dark and murkey and misty swamp, running from an unknown animal.

My four crazy chocolate labs are lots of fun when we walk through the woods.

Fringed Moccasins and Wooly Arms: Using Describing Words

The following mini-lesson idea is one of my favorites for helping young writers take a first step toward writing with detail. It is effective because the only extra effort required of the student is to add just one more word.

I gather my students around me and ask them to close their eyes and picture "fingertips." Next, I ask them to picture red-painted fingertips. As they open their eyes I ask, "which sentence gave you greater detail in your mind?" They unanimously agree that *red-painted fingertips* painted a better picture with words than just plain *fingertips*. We repeat this process for *moccasins* and *fringed moccasins, arms* and *wooly arms, views* and *city views*. We pause after each word pair to marvel at the difference just one word makes when it comes to adding greater detail.

I copy the descriptions at right from *The Purple Coat* on chart paper to further exemplify how a few extra words can help readers get a clearer picture of what the writer intended the reader to see.

To give students a chance to write similar descriptive language, I copy individual words onto slips of paper, place them in my "emerald coat" pocket and invite students to choose one. I copy enough words so that everyone has one. I copy some of the words twice, in order to show that two writers may describe the same object in different ways.

The results of the students' efforts prove that adding a few carefully chosen words can make a difference in writing with detail. Below is some of the delightfully descriptive language my students created using the words from our coat pocket.

- bright golden shades of pumpkin
- suede-patched elbows
- smudge-glass
- fat sandwich
- long, dark passageways
- city shopping
- ancient, rattly windows
- important-looking calendar
- wheels that hiss and screech
- tiny tangerine buttons
- big gold buttons
- her worried voice

Words from Our Coat Pocket

puppy	pencil
book	crayon
Grandma	sneaker
cat	eyes
car	bowl of spaghetti
dress	tree
door	wallpaper

Just a Few More Words

floppy-eared puppy with a wagging tail
chocolate brown eyes
bright sky-blue eyes
faded sneaker with untied laces
squeaky new sneakers
pointy-tipped crayon
dull crayon with a torn-paper tip
dripping bowl of spaghetti
huggable Grandma
brand new never-been-opened book
worn-out book with bent corners on the cover
freshly painted front door
thick wooden door with a shiny brass plate

Grampa, Gabrielle, and Pastrami: Studying Consonant Blends

The text of *The Purple Coat* lends itself well to a mini-lesson on consonant blends. Read a page at a time from the story, giving emphasis to those words that contain blends. Students record *The Purple Coat's* consonant blends onto a recording sheet or chalkboard as you write the words on the board. Depending on your students' abilities, you may wish to have students listen for words with blends at the beginning, in the middle, or at the end of the word rather than listening for all words with blends. On another day, students might wave a hand to signal they heard a word with a blend at the beginning, in the middle, or at the end of a word. Or make a class chart such as the one shown below. This activity works well when you want to put a few extra minutes to good use while waiting for a guest speaker or the buses to arrive.

The Purple Coat's Consonant Blends

Beginning Blends	Blends in the Middle	Blends at the End
start	Gabrielle	fast
Grampa	express	past
treasures	distant	hungry
close	between	
pressed	answers	
smudge	fabric	
station	whispers	
train	pastrami	
fringed	extras	
street	complains	
crosstown	underground	
Broadway		
screech		
crowded		

Character Report Cards: Evaluating Character Traits

At the beginning of the story, Gabby decides to stick with something she knows she likes—salami. By the end of the story she feels that "once in a while it's good to try something new." This change demonstrates progress on Gabby's part in the area of "flexibility." If Gabby were being graded on this trait, her grade would demonstrate positive growth. Share one or more of the report cards shown below; then invite your students complete a report card of their own.

Ask students to review Gabby, Mama, or Grampa's actions in *The Purple Coat*, looking for various positive traits such as kindness, flexibility, or respect. Students list these traits as subjects, using copies of the Character Report Card found on page 35. (Depending on the ability of students, you may either assign the specific traits or allow students to supply them.) Students then decide on an appropriate grade according to the character's actions in the story. Remind students to include written comments to support each grade given.

Character Report Card

Character's Name: Gabrielle

Grade: A   **Subject Area:** Flexibility

Comments: Even though Gabby wanted to stick to salami in her sandwich, she wanted to try something new and get a purple coat instead of the navy blue she usually chooses. She is showing improvement in this area.

Character Report Card

Character's Name: Grampa

Grade: A   **Subject Area:** Fairness

Comments: He reminded Mama of the tangerine dress she wanted when she was a little girl to help her understand Gabby's need for a purple coat. His idea to include a navy blue side helps Mama and Gabby feel better about the purple coat.

The Perfect Coat: Designing Original Creations

In this art activity, students have the opportunity to design their own perfect coat. What color will it be? Is it long or short, hooded, unhooded, with extra big pockets or built-in mitten clips? Does it have special buttons or snaps or a specially designed zipper guaranteed to not get stuck? Pointing out that what's perfect for one student may not be for another helps students learn to accept individual differences.

Simply stock the art center with lots of crayons, markers, or perhaps paints and brushes. butcher paper could be used to make life-size patterns of the coats. Hang these perfect coats in the hallway with brief descriptions written by the designers.

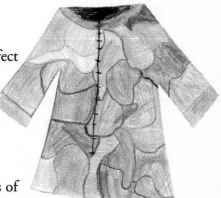

A Perfect Coat

Purple on One Side, Navy on the Other: Resolving Conflicts Through Compromise

For those days when Gabby didn't quite feel like purple, Grampa suggested that her coat be purple on one side and navy on the other. Give your students an opportunity to practice the art of compromise. Divide the class into groups of three to four to brainstorm possible solutions to situations such as those described below using the characters from *The Purple Coat*. Each group should agree on one compromise from their list of possible solutions. You may wish to give different situations to each group or one for all groups to ponder. Encourage creative compromising, as demonstrated by this sample situation and compromise:

☀ **Situation:** Mama tells Gabby her fringed moccasins are no longer fit to wear. These are Gabby's favorite shoes!

☀ **Compromise:** Allow Gabby to wear the moccasins around the house and for playing in but insist she wear a better pair of shoes when appropriate—to the city, to a friend's house, etc. (Gabby might also point out that Grampa always wears the same green sweater and wonder why she isn't allowed to wear the same fringed moccasins.)

More Situations to Ponder

☀ **Situation:** As a perfect way to end their special day in the city, Mama and Gabby want to take Grampa to a Broadway show to celebrate. Gabby wants to see *Beauty and the Beast* again, but Grampa and Mama want to see *The Lion King*. There are tickets available for both shows.

☀ **Situation:** Gabby and Grampa have a disagreement over the color of her coat lining. Grampa says the purple lining fabric doesn't match. Gabby thinks it does match.

☀ **Situation:** The next time they go into the city, Gabby takes her friend. On the train, they have a disagreement about who gets to sit next to the smudge-glass window.

☀ **Situation:** Next year, Gabby insists on a scarlet red coat. Mama still wants a navy blue coat and Grampa thinks she should have a dark green coat for a change.

Map of the City: Designing a Community

Grampa's city tailor shop or "Abe Fine-Fine Tailoring," as it says on the door of his shop, is just one necessary part of the community in which he lives. The corner deli, Mama's city shops, and the subway station are also mentioned in *The Purple Coat*. Bring this book to a social studies lesson on community and invite students to help you compile a list of the other places needed to make this community complete. Schools, grocery stores, gas stations, churches, synagogues, parks, and doctors' offices are just a few of the places students should include in their lists. Have students work alone or in teams to draw a city map that includes all the necessary places.

▲ *Tyler's City Map*

What Every Community Needs

hospital	grocery store	restaurants
doctor's office	park	post office
dentist	places to live	bank
school	church	synagogue
gas station	library	shops

More Books by Amy Hest

Baby Duck and the Bad Eyeglasses (Candlewick Press, 1996)

* *The Crack of Dawn Walkers* (Macmillan Publishing Company, 1984)

Gabby Growing Up (Simon & Schuster Books for Young Readers, 1998)

In the Rain with Baby Duck (Candlewick Press, 1995)

Nana's Birthday Party (Morrow Junior Books, 1993)

When Jessie Came Across the Sea (Candlewick Press, 1997)

* This book is out of print. Try to obtain a copy in a local or school library.

Name _____ Date _____

Measuring Me!

I am measuring with _____.

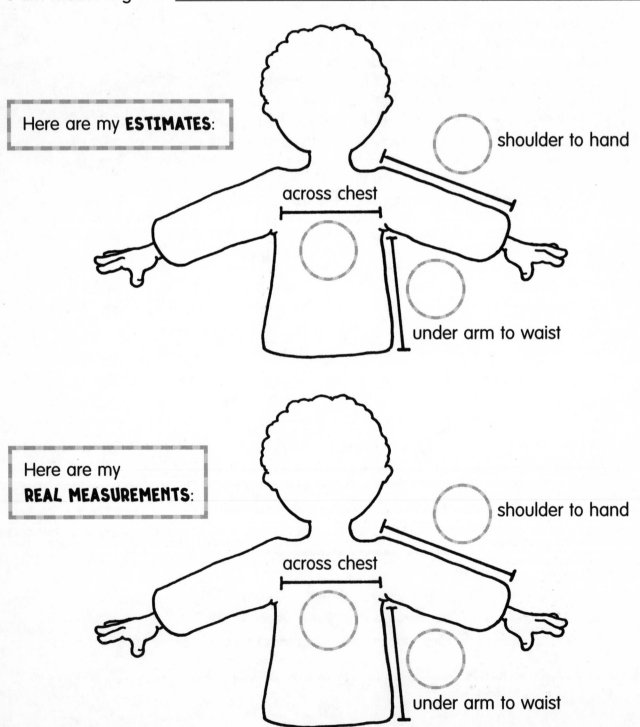

Here are my **ESTIMATES**:

shoulder to hand

across chest

under arm to waist

Here are my
REAL MEASUREMENTS:

shoulder to hand

across chest

under arm to waist

Name _____ Date _____

Character Report Card

☆ A. Fine School District ☆

Dear _____,

This report card reflects your progress made in the story <u>The Purple Coat</u>.
Your growth throughout the story has been taken into account when assigning the following grades.

(A) Outstanding Progress   (B) Good Progress   (C) Satisfactory Progress   (D) Little Progress   (F) No Progress

Grade _____ Subject Area _____

Comments: _____

_____

_____

_____

_____

Grade _____ Subject Area _____

Comments: _____

_____

_____

_____

_____

Adapted from *Literacy Through Literature*, by Terry D. Johnson and Daphne R. Louis, Heinemann, 1987 & Instructor Magazine, August, 1999.

Chapter Three

All My Favorite Things, Please!

LESSONS 21 TO 30
Yoko
by Rosemary Wells

Mini-Lessons Across the Curriculum

Language Arts

Favorite Recipes	*Creating a class book*
Alike and Different	*Comparing and contrasting character traits*
Menu Writing	*Improving spelling*
Mango Smoothies, Potato Knishes, and Cream Cheese Sandwiches	*Identifying words with -sh, -ch, and -th*

Math & Science

Lunch Box Math	***Estimating and counting objects to 100***
All Our Favorite Snacks	*Practicing estimating and counting objects to 100*
Graphing All Our Favorite Things	*Making bar graphs*
Timothy and Yoko's Sushi Shop	*Counting coins*

Community

That's Our Motto	*Writing a class motto*

Art

Clay Sushi	*Rolling, shaping, and cutting clay*

Lunch Box Math

GOAL *Estimating and Counting Objects to 100*

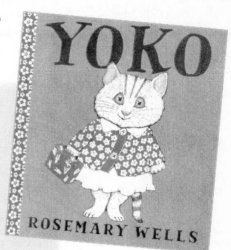

" 'What would you like for lunch today, my little cherry
blossom?' asked Yoko's mother.
'All my favorite things, please,' answered Yoko.
Yoko's mother spread steamed rice on a bamboo mat. She
rolled up a secret treasure inside each piece. Then she packed
it all in a willow-covered cooler. "

~ *Yoko* by Rosemary Wells, pp. 3–4.

The first time I opened *Yoko* and saw the patterned rows of
sushi, a math lesson immediately sprang to mind. I knew my
students would love counting the neatly made pieces of sushi.
So, when it was time for such a lesson, Yoko and "all her
favorite things" helped us with another successful mini-lesson.

This estimating and counting lesson helps students develop number sense
by giving them hands-on experience with numbers. By counting 40 objects
from our favorite lunch, for example, students have a better understanding
of what 40 really is. Estimating or guessing prior to actually counting gives
students a basis from which to compare numbers—"I guessed that amount
of grapes was 45 but it's only 28." Concrete math experiences improve
young children's math confidence as well as their understanding of numbers.

As you will see in the mini-lesson that follows, as students practice
estimating, their ability to talk about numbers and the reasoning behind
ideas becomes more sophisticated—even after only one lesson. Enlist a
parent volunteer to help with the preparations listed below. The students'
success and excitement for the lesson make these few extra steps worthwhile.
To prepare for this lesson:

☼ Gather snacks needed for this lesson (see the teaching tip on page 38).

☼ Make copies of a recording sheet like the model shown on page 42 and
copy for each student.

There are several ways to collect snack items for this lesson. You may have a Party Parent whose job is to contact other parents for treat donations. You may send a note home to either a few parents or to all parents. The latter will most likely provide your class with a stash of snacks to kick-off future lessons or to use as special treats.

If you don't want to use "real" favorite lunch items, have a parent volunteer assemble "look-alike" treats using items found in the classroom. Marbles could be placed in a baggie and labeled as "grapes," green pattern blocks could be labeled as potato chips, and orange crayons could be carrot sticks, for example.

☀ Assemble individual lunch baggies, using the snack items. Ask student to form pairs. Ask each pair to first estimate and then count the contents of one baggie during the "independent practice" segment of the lesson. Label the baggies to coordinate with your recording sheet.

☀ Collect items for a sample favorite lunch. Organize snack items so that students can compare the same amounts of different items—42 peanut butter crackers with 42 grapes, for example. My typical "favorite things" lunch for estimating numbers to 100 includes:

- carrot sticks (about 21+)
- peanut butter crackers (42)
- baggie of peanut M&M's for a special treat (about 65)
- grapes (42)

☀ Assign math partners or groups for individual practice time or have students form pairs.

☀ Gather counting cups to organize the items into groups of tens when counting.

With these preparations complete, I settle in front of the class holding up my lunch box, ready for a math lesson inspired by *Yoko*.

Mrs. L.:	This morning as I was packing my lunch, I asked myself "What would I like for lunch today?" So I decided to pack all my favorite things.
Madison:	That's just what Yoko's mother packed for her.
Mrs. L.:	Exactly.
Collin:	It's called sushi.
Mrs. L.:	Inside Yoko's willow-covered cooler are the pieces of sushi her mother packed for her. I'd like you to look at the picture for a moment; then I'll close the book and ask you to tell me without counting how many pieces you think were inside the cooler. You will be giving me your best guess—an estimate of how much sushi Yoko has.
Hannah:	But we aren't supposed to count them?
Mrs. L.:	No. Look at the sushi inside the willow-covered cooler and make your best guess. Remember, when you are estimating, you probably won't guess the exact number; your goal is to be within a reasonable range of that number.
Jack:	How close to the real number do we have to be? Five numbers away?
Mrs. L.:	That would be excellent.
Jack:	But 50 numbers off would not be a very good estimate, would it?
Mrs. L.:	With practice, I'm sure your estimates will be closer to the exact number than 50. When you estimate, you have to think reasonably. For example, would it be reasonable to assume that Yoko would eat 100 pieces of sushi for lunch?

David:	No, because she wouldn't have time to eat that much during lunch time at school.
Tyler:	And 100 wouldn't fit in her lunch box.
Courtney:	And 100 pieces of sushi would probably make her sick!
Mrs. L.:	This is logical or reasonable thinking. Would her mother pack just 2 pieces of sushi?
Molly:	If they are the size of sandwiches, maybe. But sushi is small, isn't it?
Emma:	I'm not a very good guesser when it comes to numbers.
Mrs. L.:	As with most things, the more you practice, the better you become. With this in mind, let's practice estimating by looking at this picture of Yoko enjoying her favorite things for lunch.

I open *Yoko* to page 10, where Yoko is eating her lunch of sushi, just long enough for students to get a glance inside Yoko's lunch box.

Mrs. L.:	Raise your hand to tell me how many pieces of sushi you think are inside Yoko's lunch.
Elizabeth:	Maybe 30. Maybe not exactly but close to it, I think.
Mrs. L.:	This sounds like a reasonable estimate. Let's have some other estimates.
Eric:	16.
Samantha:	20.
Emma:	18.
Jack:	10.
Matthew:	About 15.
Mrs. L.:	These are all good estimates. You guess that there are between 10 and 30 pieces of sushi. Let's look at the page again to check our estimate by counting the favorite things in Yoko's lunch box.

We count 19 pieces inside the box.

David:	Yoko is getting ready to eat another piece so that would make 20.
Alex:	That's the second piece she has eaten. She already ate an orange piece.
Mrs. L.:	Looks like it to me, too.
Samantha:	That would be 21! My estimate was close—I guessed 20!
Mrs. L.:	What excellent estimating! In fact, all of your estimates or guesses were very close.
Emma:	And we didn't get much time to look at the picture.
Mrs. L.:	You're right. Now we are going to do some more estimating. I've packed a lunch of a few of my favorite things just for math. First I'd like you to help me estimate how many items are in each baggie. Then we'll actually count the items together. I've also gathered some counting cups and other items to help us with this project.
Courtney:	What are your favorite things for lunch, Mrs. Lunsford?
Mrs. L.:	Let's take a look in the bag and find out. Courtney, why don't you reach inside and choose one of my favorite things, please?

Courtney:	Carrots.
Madison:	They are good for you.
Lauren:	You sure packed a lot of them!
Mrs. L.:	Tell me how many you think a lot is without actually counting the carrots. Take your best guess and I'll start jotting your estimates on the board.

Students make estimates and I record them.

Mrs. L.:	So our estimates are anywhere from 15 to 30. Eric, please count the carrots in my favorite lunch.
Eric:	Sure! 1, 2, 3, … 22.
Mrs. L.:	Good counting, Eric. I don't see number 22 on our list of estimates.
Lauren:	Maybe we should count them one more time to make sure Eric didn't make a mistake.
Mrs. L.:	Eric was a very careful counter but it never hurts to check your work a second time, does it? Let's count by 2's this time….
Class:	2, 4, 6, 8, … 22.
Mrs. L.:	Which number on our list of estimates comes closest to the actual number of carrots?
Tori:	23. That was my guess.
Courtney:	So does 21.
Mrs. L.:	Yes, since 22 is in between 21 and 23, both of these guesses are closest to the actual number of carrots. All of your estimates are very close to the actual number of carrots. More excellent estimating! Let's test your estimating skills with another item from my favorite lunch. Mary, would you choose something, please.
Mary:	Peanut butter crackers.
Tori:	The mini-sized ones. You can get more of them in your baggie than the carrots because they are smaller.
Mrs. L.:	How many crackers do you estimate are in my lunch?

Students again contribute estimates, which I record.

Mrs. L.:	Any others? Then your range of estimates for the peanut butter crackers is between 25 and 50. Let's use counting cups to count these crackers. Let's have two volunteers carefully count out groups of ten crackers to place ten into counting cups.

Students count the crackers; there are 42.

David:	Nobody guessed 42.
Mrs. L.:	What was the closest estimate?
Emma:	46, I think.
Madison:	No, 40 is closer because it's only 2 away from 42.
Emma:	46 is four away from 42.
Mrs. L.:	Good math thinking. There was a greater range of estimates for the crackers. Any idea why?

Samantha: Maybe because there were more things to guess and it was harder to guess the number.

Tyler: There were more numbers to choose from.

Mrs. L.: I agree. There are two more items in my favorite things lunch.

Molly: I'll pick something to count…Here are some M&M's!

Mrs. L.: Take a look at the amount of M&M's in my lunch. Do you think I have enough to share with all of you?

Tori: We could probably all have just one M&M. I bet there are 21 in the baggie.

Collin: I think there are enough for all of us to have two apiece.

Matthew: That would be 42.

Stephanie: That's how many crackers we had. Since the M&M's are smaller, there must be more than 42. The bag of M&M's looks like it has more in it than the crackers.

Mrs. L.: So what are your estimates?

Students estimate the number of M&M's.

Stephanie: Maybe there's enough for 3 each…that would be 63.

Mrs. L.: How did you get that number so fast?

Stephanie: Well, I counted by 2's and added a zero for the tens…20, 40, 60. Then, since there are 21 students, I counted the one three times and got 3 ones—63.

Mrs. L.: Excellent thinking, Stephanie. Any other estimates?

Madison: My guess is somewhere around 60, too.

Mrs. L.: So, your estimates are in a range from 50 to 70. How should we count these M&M's?

Ben: I would use the counting cups and count the tens by 2's.

Mrs. L.: That's a clever idea. Let's do it together. Ben, you come up and move the M&M's into cups while we help you count.

We count by 2's and Ben places groups of 10 M&M's in cups

Ben: There are 65!

David: We each get three M&M's! And there are two left over.

Stephanie: I was close—I guessed 63.

Mrs. L.: That is an excellent estimate—within a range of two. There should be one other thing in my favorite lunch to estimate.

Jack: Just grapes are left.

Mrs. L.: Do you think there will be more or less grapes than there were M&M's?

We discuss the size of the grapes and make our estimates.

Mrs. L.: I think that's a good span of numbers—between 38 and 50. Let's count the grapes…by 2's.

Tori: I'll put them into counting cups.

Class: 2, 4, 6, 8, 10, 12, 14…42.

Mary: 42 is the same number as the peanut butter crackers.

Mrs. L.: So here is what 42 looks like in grapes, and here is what it looks like in mini peanut butter crackers. There are 21 carrot sticks. Forty-two is 21 and 21 more.

Alex: So there are twice as many grapes and peanut butter crackers as there are carrot sticks.

Stephanie: And three times as many M&M's as there are carrot sticks.

Madison: Right, because 21 three times is 63.

Mrs. L.: Once again, I must say I am impressed with your estimating skills. The next time you have to work with the number 42, think of these crackers and grapes. Think of the 21 carrot sticks, and the 65 M&M's. You have a picture in your mind of what these numbers look like. Now that we know just how many of each treat is in my favorite lunch, I know how many will be fair to share. Estimates give you a rough idea, counting gives you exact numbers. After a little more estimating practice, we'll enjoy a little after-math snack.

NOTE: Be sure to check for food allergies before sharing these favorite snacks.

Independent Practice

All Our Favorite Snacks: Practicing Estimating and Counting Objects to 100

Mrs. L.: To give you a little extra practice with estimating, I've prepared some snacks for you to estimate and count. In each numbered lunch bag there is a stack of counting cups and a favorite snack. You and your math partner will choose a snack bag and use this Favorite Snacks recording sheet to record your estimates and the actual number of items counted for each snack bag. For example, if you choose snack bag #4, you will look inside and see that you will be estimating Goldfish crackers.

Sam: Can we eat them?

A Favorite Snacks Recording Sheet ▶

All Our Favorite Snacks
☆ A math lesson on estimating and counting ☆

	My Estimate	I Counted
Snack Bag 1		
Snack Bag 2		
Snack Bag 3		
Snack Bag 4		
Snack Bag 5		
Snack Bag 6		
Snack Bag 7		
Snack Bag 8		
Snack Bag 9		
Snack Bag 10		
Snack Bag 11		
Snack Bag 12		

Mrs. L.:	No, because everyone needs to have a chance to count all the items. Remember, you will be having Lunch Box snacks after our estimating practice. Fair enough?	
Class:	Yes!	
Mrs. L.:	On the recording sheet, locate the bag you and your partner are using. First record your estimate of how many items you think are in the bag.	

▲ *Counting Our Favorite Snacks*

Elizabeth:	We need to write the estimate down before we count, right?
Mrs. L.:	Yes. If I see partners counting, I should be able to glance at their recording sheets to see their estimate. Remember an estimate is your...
Class:	Best guess!
Mrs. L.:	That means you shouldn't expect to get the estimate exactly the same as the counted number.
Stephanie:	And we aren't supposed to change our estimate to make it look like we guessed perfectly.
Ben:	But we should be within a pretty close range of that number.
Mrs. L.:	Good luck! Let's start estimating and counting.

Our Lunch Box Estimates
▼

Yoko's Sushi

30	18
16	10
20	15

● We counted 20

Carrot Sticks

20	23	18
30	24	21
25	28	15

● We counted 22

Peanut Butter Crackers

28	40	39
38	33	46
25	50	

● We counted 42

M&M's

50	70
55	60
58	63

● We counted 65

Grapes

50	45	47
55	39	
38	43	

● We counted 42

8 More Book-Based Lessons

 ## Graphing All Our Favorite Things: Making Bar Graphs

For a fun graphing lesson, make a picture bar graph using Yoko and her classmates' favorite lunches. Label a large sheet of butcher paper with the title "All Our Favorite Things, Please!" Next, record the names and simplified pictures of the lunches found on pages 8 and 9 of *Yoko* (see pages 50 and 51 for reproducibles) vertically or horizontally across the chart paper. Include Timothy's peanut butter and honey sandwich, Valerie's cream cheese and jelly, Fritz's meatball grinder, Tulip's Swiss cheese on rye, Hazel's egg salad on pumpernickel, Doris' squeeze cheese on white, the Franks' franks and beans and, of course, Yoko's sushi.

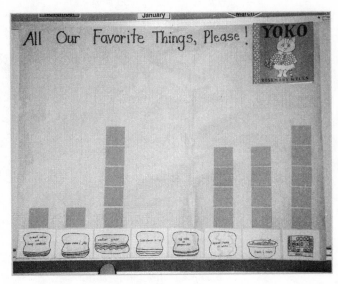

▲ *Our "Favorite Things" Graph*

Display the graph near a gathering space. Give each student a sticky note and have them write their name on the front. Review the favorite lunches of Yoko and her classmates then discuss how everyone's different likes and dislikes make them special. Next, have students choose which favorite lunch they would most like to try—no "yuks, blaahs, or oohs" are allowed as students make their selections. After the last student has added a marker to the graph, discuss the results of the graph, with "Tell-Me" statements such as:

☀ Tell me about the three most popular lunch choices.

☀ Tell me about the least popular lunch choices.

☀ Tell me a fact about the graph using the word "more."

☀ Tell me a fact about the graph using the word "less."

☀ Tell me a fact about the graph using a number word.

☀ Tell me a fact about the graph using addition.

That's Our Motto: Writing a Class Motto

Each new school year, I ask students to decide upon a class motto to help create a desirable classroom atmosphere. I ask students to put themselves in Yoko's shoes at lunch, snack time, and on International Food Day when her classmates made fun of her favorite things. From there, we talk about the kind of classroom atmosphere we want in Room 4. We make a list of possible mottoes, stressing positive actions rather than negative ones. The words "We all get along" take care of potential problems such as "We don't hit," and "We don't push," for example.

After plenty of ideas have been generated, I explain that we will be voting on the class motto to be displayed and followed in the classroom for the entire school year. To prepare for the election, I copy each potential motto onto a sentence strip and place a paper cup under each. Students vote for their favorite motto by placing a marker (such as a Unifix cube) in the cup under their selection. Together, we count the markers and proclaim our new class motto. The next day, as the students enter the classroom, our new motto is ready to be signed and displayed in a prominent place. Some of the mottoes my students have supported in years past are shown at right.

In Room 4,

- ☀ We all get along.
- ☀ We like each other.
- ☀ We treat others the way we would like to be treated.
- ☀ We always do our best.
- ☀ We are kind to one another.
- ☀ We are friendly.

Clay Sushi: Rolling, Shaping, and Cutting Clay

Using the text and illustrations from page 4 of *Yoko* as a guide, I set up an art center for making clay sushi—just like Yoko's mother made for her. I gather an assortment of clay, "bamboo mats" made of paper, paper scraps, rice and glitter for "secret treasures," and plastic knives for cutting. I mark page 4 of *Yoko* and place the book at the art center for reference during sushi-making. After reading the page aloud, I demonstrate the sushi-making technique, then invite students to make their own sushi at this center during their free time. I provide shoe boxes as "willow-covered coolers" and ask the students to place their sushi in the boxes to be served at "Timothy and Yoko's Sushi Shop" (see page 46).

▲ *Demonstrating Our Sushi-Making Technique*

Timothy and Yoko's Sushi Shop: Counting Coins

"On the bus Timothy and Yoko made plans to push their desks together and open a restaurant the very next day."

~page 31, *Yoko*

To give students practice with counting quarters, nickels, dimes, and pennies (or any combination of coins your students may be working with), I designate an area near the art center as "Timothy and Yoko's Sushi Shop." I cover a small table with a craft paper tablecloth, add a plastic vase filled with silk flowers, paper plates, and plastic utensils and we're open for business! Patrons order delicious clay sushi made at the art center then pay the wait staff using plastic coins. A menu displaying prices that correspond with students' counting goals hangs nearby (see activity below). Explain that any money counting concerns should be taken up with the manager (teacher!).

Menu Writing: Improving Spelling

During a writers' workshop mini-lesson, students and I make a menu to display at Timothy and Yoko's Sushi Shop. While students enjoy inventing creative names for their clay sushi creations, they are also getting much needed spelling practice. Students name their creations as I say the words slowly (K-rrrrr-iiii-sss-p-eee) asking them to call out the letter sounds they hear. I write the letters they say on the board as "sound-spelling." Providing lap boards for students to practice the spelling of each word along with me gives students greater participation in the lesson.

After the menu of sound-spelled words is complete, I record the "book-spelling" beside the sound-spelled words. *Pnkst shrmp* becomes *pinkest shrimp*, for example, and *krab kons* becomes *crab cones*. We discuss any spelling rules encountered such as *y* makes the sound of *e* at the end of words, and the silent 'e' and two vowels walking together rules.

Finally, I ask a volunteer to copy our book-spelled menu onto a lap-sized chalkboard. We add prices based on our present money counting goals (counting coins to fifty cents and below) before displaying the menu near "Timothy and Yoko's Sushi Shop." Using a chalkboard allows us to change the prices of items and add items to our menu as often as we like.

Favorite Recipes:
Creating a Class Book

A few years ago, my students and I put together a recipe book as a keepsake for our student teacher. The book was a success, so I had copies made for the students to take home as well as a few to share with school helpers in our building. Now, "Favorite Recipes from Room 4" has become a yearly tradition and one that fits perfectly with our lessons based on *Yoko*.

I send a letter to parents requesting a copy of one of their child's favorite recipes. Attached to the parent letter is a "recipe card," an 8 1/2 x 11 piece of paper with a recipe heading. Parents and children work together to copy the recipe onto the card and return it to school. If the recipe is long, I invite parents to photocopy it and tape it to the card. A space is provided for the young chef's photo and any illustrations they may wish to include.

After all the recipes have been returned (this often requires reminder notes or phone calls to a few parents), we assemble the recipes alphabetically by chef's name (you may wish to do this by food categories). Students work together on the cover illustrations, making cooking-related pencil drawings to glue on the book cover. I make several copies of our original book for students to sign out and take home to share with parents, try a few recipes, and perhaps make a copy of the book to keep.

◀ *The First Edition of Our Cookbook*

One Chef's Favorite Recipe
▼

Alike and Different: Comparing and Contrasting Character Traits

To help your students appreciate that each class member is unique, invite them to interview each other. Give partners copies of the "Meet My Friend" recording sheet found on page 52. Invite students to take individual clipboards or lap boards, pencils, and crayons off to a private spot in the classroom to conduct their interviews. After students have finished making discoveries, meet as a class to have partners share one way they are alike and one way they are different from their interviewed friend. Or, have students write stories based upon the likes and differences they discovered through the interview process. These stories, with an added illustration of the new friend, make a wonderful display for an Open House or during conference time with parents.

▲ *Interviewing Friends*

Meet a Friend
▼

Mango Smoothies, Potato Knishes, and Cream Cheese Sandwiches: Identifying Words With -<u>sh</u>, -<u>ch</u>, -<u>th</u>

Yoko provides an excellent opportunity to have your students identify and/or classify words containing the sounds -*th* and -*sh* and -*ch*. This quick lesson gives young readers and writers practice with these often confusing sounds and helps them commit these letter-sound relationships to memory. Simply copy these digraphs onto three separate charts as shown on page 49. If you'd like, copy headings for beginning, middle, and end of words as well.

As you read the story of *Yoko*, students give a signal each time they hear a word that belongs on one of the charts. Depending on your students' abilities, you may wish to have them listen for one, two, or all three of the digraphs at once. This is a great lesson to occupy free minutes at the end of the day and the charts allow for additional words to be added from other sources.

TH

beginning of word		middle of word		end of word
things	thermos	mother	together	Timothy
then	than	everything	anything	with
the	they	smoothies		
that's				

SH

beginning of word	middle of word	end of word
shrimp	sushi	fish
show	knishes	dish
		Irish
		polish-ed
		push

CH

beginning of word	middle of word	end of word
cherry	enchiladas	lunch
cheese	pitcher	sandwich
chopsticks		watch
choice		switch-ed
		touch-ed

More Books by Rosemary Wells

Benjamin and Tulip (Random House, 1973)

Bunny Cakes (Puffin Books, 1997)

Bunny Money (Dial Books for Young Readers, 1997)

Emily's First 100 Days of School (Hyperion Books for Children, 2000)

First Tomato: A Voyage to the Bunny Planet (Dial Books for Young Readers, 1992)

Fritz and the Mess Fairy (Dial Books for Young Readers, 1991)

Max Cleans Up (Viking Children's Books, 2000)

Max's Dragon Shirt (Dial Books for Young Readers, 1991)

McDuff Moves In (Hyperion Books for Children, 1997)

Morris's Disappearing Bag—A Christmas Story (The Dial Press, 1975)

Noisy Nora (Hyperion Books for Children, 1998)

Read to Your Bunny (Scholastic, 1997)

Timothy Goes to School (Dial Books for Young Readers, 1981)

Waiting for the Evening Star (Dial Books for Young Readers, 1993)

Graphing All Our Favorite Things

cream cheese
& jelly

swiss cheese
on rye

peanut butter
& honey

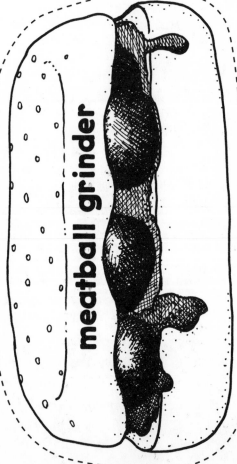

meatball grinder

100 Skill-Building Lessons Using 10 Favorite Books   Scholastic Professional Books

☆ Graphing All Our Favorite Things ☆

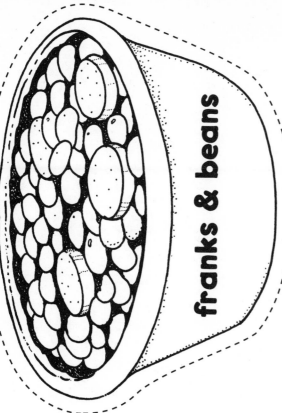

franks & beans

squeeze cheese on white

egg salad on pumpernickel

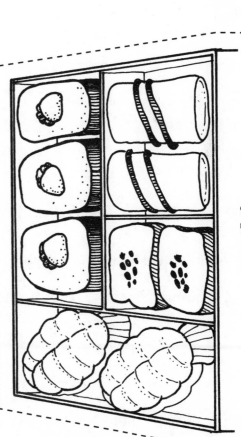

sushi

Meet My Friend

Here is my
friend's picture.

My name is _____.

This is my friend _____.

My friend has _____ eyes.

My friend has _____ hair.

My friend's favorite color is _____.

My friend's favorite thing to do at school is _____.

My friend has _____ pets.

Their names are _____.

My friend is good at _____

and wants to improve at _____.

In my friend's free time, he/she enjoys _____.

When my friend grows up, he/she hopes to be a _____.

One thing that is the same about my friend and me is _____

_____.

One thing that is different about my friend and me is _____

_____.

100 Skill-Building Lessons Using 10 Favorite Books   Scholastic Professional Books

Chapter Four

I Wish I Were Still Back in Bed

LESSONS 31 TO 40
Arthur's Teacher Trouble
by Marc Brown

Mini-Lessons Across the Curriculum

Language Arts

The Test Will Have One Hundred Words	*Improving spelling techniques*
Weekly Spelling Words	*Practicing spelling with "tips and tricks"*
A Team Spellathon	*Spelling practice*
Words in Our Memory Banks	*Making personal dictionaries*
What Dictionary Are You Using?	*Sharpening dictionary skills*

Math & Science

How Much Is 100?	*Estimating items to 100*

Community

Prunella Loses, Arthur Wins	*Discussing sportsmanship*
Quiet Places to Study	*Discussing good study habits*

Art

Marc Brown's Borders	*Reviewing patterns*
Arthur's House	*Making details count*

The Test Will Have One Hundred Words

GOAL *Improving Spelling Techniques*

 The next day, Mr. Ratburn announced a spelling test for Friday. 'I want you to study very hard,' he said. 'The test will have a hundred words.' Buster looked pale. 'And,' continued Mr. Ratburn, 'the two students with the highest scores will represent our class at the all-school spellathon.' "

~*Arthur's Teacher Trouble* by Marc Brown, pp. 10–11.

T he idea of a test is intimidating to many first, second, and third graders, and the thought of having to spell words with book spelling is often frustrating. After reading *Arthur's Teacher Trouble*, students realize that, with effort, learning to spell words as they appear in books does have its rewards and can even be fun.

Allowing students to write using sound or phonetic spelling is valuable to young children. Sound spelling builds confidence in language skills, gives students a sense of independence in written language communication, and provides a connection of those sounds heard orally to written form. Sound spelling is essential during writers' workshop, for spelling should not interfere with a creative writing idea. However, frustration often results when students discover that words they struggled to sound out are spelled differently in books. When done diplomatically, pointing out the difference between phonetic and conventional spelling goes a long way in helping students commit conventional spelling to memory.

Each school year, I gently explain that one of the best ways to become a better speller is to read, read, read. I add, with a smile, that a new word must be read hundreds of times before it is committed to memory. I offer empathy for their frustration then read *Arthur's Teacher Trouble* for read-aloud. Our lesson continues as I share a few helpful spelling tricks and tips plus a touch of silliness based on this favorite book. To prepare for the lesson, I make a transparency of the "Spelling Tips and Tricks" found on page 66 as well as copies of "My Weekly Spelling Words" (model on page 60) and the letter to parents (page 67). With these preparations complete, we gather for a mini-lesson that introduces a few spelling tricks and tips to prevent students from wishing they were still back in bed on the day their first spelling test of the year is announced.

Mrs. L.:	On Friday, we will be having our first spelling test of the school year. I want you to study very hard. The test will have one hundred words.
Alex:	That sounds familiar.
Tori:	That's what Mr. Ratburn told Arthur's class.
Madison:	Are we really having a spelling test?
Anna:	Is it really going to have 100 words?
Mrs. L.:	Yes and no. Yes, we are having a spelling test—but it won't have 100 words. The expressions on your faces look like Arthur and his classmates' on this page of *Arthur's Teacher Trouble* (I open the book to pages 10–11). Relax, boys and girls. By Friday, I'm sure you will all be ready for your spelling test. We will practice just like Arthur and his classmates did.
Molly:	Why can't we just use sound spelling forever?
Tori:	There is a real way to write words.
Courtney:	Anyway, I can't always read my sound spelling after I've written it.
Mrs. L.:	You've just figured out why we need to learn book spelling. Writing is a way of communicating with ourselves and each other. When we write something down on paper, it needs to be able to be read again at another time. If we can't remember what we wanted to say, the idea is forgotten.
Anna:	Sometimes I can't read my writing because it's messy.
Mrs. L.:	Then we should work on being neat spellers, as well. Learning to spell so that you can share ideas with others is important. Sound spelling is a wonderful way to begin writing words but eventually you need to spell words like they appear in books so that you and others are able to understand your ideas. Once you learn how to spell a word, you will be able to write faster. Take your name for example. You all know book spelling for your names.
Sam:	I've been able to write my name since I was three.
Mrs. L.:	Excellent. Stephanie, can we use your name as an example?
Stephanie:	Sure.
Mrs. L.:	Let's say we have to write Stephanie's name. We start by writing an—
Samantha:	S— same as my name.
Mrs. L.:	Right. Next we need a—
Tori:	T. Stephanie starts with the st blend.
Ben:	Next is an e.

Sam:	Then an f—
Stephanie:	No, it's p-h.
Mrs. L.:	Since we're sound spelling, either of these sounds would be fine. They both make the /f/ sound.
Stephanie:	O.K.
Lauren:	Next I hear an n.
Alex:	Then an e.
Stephanie:	My name doesn't look like S-T-E-F-N-E.
Mrs. L.:	Yes, but we came up with most of the main sounds. Stephanie, would you please write your name in book spelling, please.
Stephanie:	Sure, it's S-T-E-P-H-A-N-I-E.
Matthew:	She did that really fast and she put in more letters.
Mrs. L.:	Stephanie doesn't have to stop to think about all the sounds like we do. She thinks of the whole word and since *Stephanie* is in her memory bank, book spelling pops into her mind like magic. In other words, once you've memorized book spelling for a word it's always there. You don't have to stop to sound out the word sound by sound. Today I'm going show you some strategies for remembering the book spelling of words. As I was reading *Arthur's Teacher Trouble* to you, I noticed many different ways Arthur's classmates practiced words. Let me show you that page.
Madison:	Arthur's reading a dictionary.
Ben:	Francine is reading a book of "Spelling Tricks and Tips."
Samantha:	Muffy is on the computer.
Sam:	Buster is buying a lucky charm.
Mrs. L.:	Sorry, I don't have any lucky charms. But I do have a book of Spelling Tricks and Tips like Francine's to share with you. I copied one of the pages onto a chart to help you practice your spelling words for the test on Friday. You may find a few of the ideas a little far-fetched, but otherwise it should be very helpful. Let's read the first spelling tip together:

Tip #1

How to learn a new word:

1. Look at the new word carefully while holding your breath.

2. Say the word 5 times as you jump up and down on one foot.

3. Spell the new word out loud, pointing to each letter in the word.

4. Close your eyes and picture the letters in the word.

5. Cover the word with a polka dot cloth then spell the word without looking.

6. Remove the cloth and spell the word again.

Repeat steps 1–6 five times for each word on your list.

Emma:	I think there are some silly ideas in there.
Mrs. L.:	I agree but they might make practicing spelling words a little more fun.
Jack:	And that might make us better spellers!
Mrs. L.:	Let's try this first tip using the words the principal used for Arthur's September Spellathon. The first word was *fear*. I'll write F-E-A-R on the board in book spelling. Try step number 1: look closely at the word *fear* while holding your breath. Next, everyone needs to stand up. While still looking at the word on the board, say *fear* five times while jumping up and down on one foot.
Class:	*Fear, fear, fear, fear, fear.*
Mrs. L.:	Nice jumping and spelling. Now, point to the letters and spell *fear* out loud.
Class:	F-E-A-R.
Mrs. L.:	Please close your eyes and picture the word *fear*.
Sam:	I'm picturing *fear* beside a lion with its mouth open.
Mrs. L.:	Nice image, Sam. Take another look at *fear*. Now, I'll cover the word with a polka-dot cloth which I brought for the occasion. You spell *fear* out loud…Open your eyes and spell it again…Smile if you spelled it correctly when you had your eyes closed. I see lots of smiles. Let's try another word.
Molly:	I think the next word at the Spellathon was *preparation*. That's a hard one.

We follow the same steps for this challenging word.

Mrs. L.:	If we take away the silly parts of this spelling tip, we will have an effective way to study words that we want to store in our memory banks. Step one should be to look at the new word carefully.
Ben:	It wouldn't hurt to say the word five times, either.
Mrs. L.:	I agree. Then what would be wise to do next?
Elizabeth:	Spell the word out loud and point to the letters.
Mrs. L.:	Then what?
Alex:	Close your eyes to see the word in your head.
Molly:	Then try to spell the word without looking.
Eric:	Spell the word one more time out loud.
Hannah:	To see if you spelled it correctly when you had your eyes closed.
Tyler:	Do this four more times for each word—five times all together.
Mrs. L.:	Great! Let's take a look at the second tip in Francine's book:

Tip #2

Use spelling clues:

1. Look and listen for little words inside the whole word (*fall*).

2. Rhyming words make spelling easier (*book, look, nook, shook, cook, hook, took*)

3. Know the vowel sounds—*a, e, i, o, u*—there is a vowel in every word.

4. Break long words into smaller parts (*Sep/tem/ber*).

5. Some words you just have to look at and remember (*friend and school*).

Stephanie: I look for little words when I'm spelling new words.

Lauren: Me, too.

Mrs. L.: This is a very important spelling clue to remember. Many long words have smaller words inside them. I'll write a few of Arthur's spelling words on the board. Please help me read the list as I write them down.

Arthur's Spelling Words

book	friend
bus	school
September	fall

Mrs. L.: Which word on his spelling test has a little word inside it?

Collin: *Fall.* It has *all* inside.

Mrs. L.: Right! If you can spell the word *all*, you can spell *fall* just by adding one more letter.

Lauren: And *ball, tall, wall.* There are lots of words with *all* inside.

Mrs. L.: Looking for little words is one of the best ways to remember the *book* spelling of words. The second clue says that rhyming words can be helpful with spelling, too. Like the word *all*, most of us know how to spell *look.*

Class: L-O-O-K.

Mrs. L.: Right. Since you can spell *look*, what other word on Arthur's list do you now how to spell?

Molly: *Book.*

Mrs. L.: Terrific. L-O-O-K and B-O-O-K.

Lauren: And *took, cook, hook*—

Anna: And *shook.*

Mrs. L.: Excellent! Tell me about the next clue: Know the vowel sounds.

David: I think that's for helping to remember words like *bus.* If you don't put in the right vowel, you wouldn't spell the word *bus*—

Ben: You might spell *bas*, or *bos.*

Emma: Arthur would probably get the *b* and *s* right. It's the vowel that's tricky.

Mrs. L.: Good thinking. This clue is all about remembering and practicing the vowel sounds. The next clue is one of my favorites for remembering longer words.

Sam: Like that long one on Arthur's list.

Tori: It's *September.*

Mrs. L.: Right. The word September could be confusing and scary to spell when you first look at it. But if you break it apart into its smaller parts—Sep-tem-ber—it's easier to spell correctly. Clap the word September with me.

We clap the word and spell each part. Then we put it all together.

Mrs. L.:	What excellent spellers you are! Now I think you are ready for a more difficult clue. Read clue number 5 with me, please.
Class:	*Some words you just have to look at and remember.*
Ben:	That's not much of a clue!
Mrs. L.:	Look at the two words left on Arthur's spelling test.
Class:	*Friend* and *school.*
Mrs. L.:	Do any of the other clues work for these words?
Eric:	*Friend* has *end* in it.
Mrs. L.:	You could use the smaller word *end* to help you spell *friend.*
Stephanie:	I say *fri-* with *-end* in my mind whenever I spell *friend.*
Courtney:	What about *school?*
Molly:	No little words.
Jack:	The vowels don't sound like real *o's.*
Hannah:	They sound like two *o's* together—*oooo.*
Mrs. L.:	Right.
Samantha:	I do hear the *sc* at the beginning of the word—
Elizabeth:	And the *l* at the end.
Emma:	But why is there an *h* in *school?*
Ben:	It must be a word we have to just look at and remember.
Mrs. L.:	I think you are right! *School* and *friend* have silent letters that make them words you have to just look at and remember.
Alex:	Or we might forget the *h* in *school* and the *i* in *friend.*
Mrs. L.:	Exactly! Let's take a look at the last spelling tip:

Tip #3

Preparing for the day of the test:

1. Practice your words at home each night.

2. Get a good night's sleep the night before the test.

3. Eat a good breakfast on the morning of the test.

4. Just before the test, spin around 3 times while saying the words "I will take my time and spell my words carefully."

Lauren:	I'll spin around three times if it will help me spell my words correctly!
Sam:	I don't think spinning will help.
Mrs. L.:	I agree. But practicing and eating and sleeping well will *do* wonders for you when it comes to spelling words with book spelling. Listen while I reread the tips from Francine's book to you. Then you will have a chance to practice spelling a few words on your own.

A Note About My Spelling Program

This mini-lesson and follow-up activity make a wonderful introduction to a formal spelling program. I selected a range of words for this lesson to give all students practice using the spelling techniques introduced in the mini-lesson. After a pretest on Monday, hands-on practice from Tuesday through Thursday, as well as independent practice at home each night, students are then tested on Friday. Typically, my students will be working on one of three spelling lists suited to ability levels.

Weekly Spelling Words: Practicing Spelling with "Tips and Tricks"

After reviewing our Spelling Tricks and Tips, I send students back to their seats to work on spelling words taken from *Arthur's Teacher Trouble*, all with the theme of school. The words you choose for your students to practice may reflect a formal spelling program, a unit of study, or words commonly misspelled by your students.

I divide my class into teams and invite them to copy our list of spelling words (shown bottom left) onto copies I have made of the spelling sheet shown below. I provide time for students to look at, jump up and down, spell the words out loud and discuss clues that might help them remember each of the words on the list. Before students leave for the day, I staple a copy of the "Parent Letter" (page 67) to the practice list to be taken home and shared with parents.

Our Take-Home Practice List ▶

My Weekly Spelling Words

1. _____   7. _____

2. _____   8. _____

3. _____   9. _____

4. _____   10. _____

5. _____   11. _____

6. _____   12. _____

Challenge Words

☆ _____

☆ _____

☆ _____

☆ _____

Our Practice List

class   name
room   test
teacher   bell
study   school

Extra Challenge Words:

principal   homework
dictionary   kindergarten

8 More Book-Based Lessons

A Team Spellathon: Spelling Practice

On Thursday afternoons, I divide the class into two teams and we have a contest similar to Arthur's Spellathon. I play the part of Mr. Ratburn, calling out words to be spelled then using each word in a sentence. One student from each team writes the word onto a lap-sized chalkboard. I ring a bell to signal time to display the chalkboards. Points are awarded to each team with a correctly spelled word.

▲ *One Afternoon Spellathon*

Prunella Loses, Arthur Wins: Discussing Sportsmanship

Use the spellathon scene from *Arthur's Teacher Trouble* to initiate a discussion of sportsmanship. Page 28 shows a disappointed Prunella and a surprised yet victorious Arthur. Have students role-play the scene between Arthur and Prunella following the spellathon. After the cheering from Mr. Ratburn's class dies down and the photographer snaps Arthur's picture, what would a good sport like Arthur say to Prunella? What would a good sport like Prunella say to Arthur? Or, have students act out the scene with one or both characters being unsportsmanlike and then depict ways for the characters to solve the problem.

Be sure to have students relate to the feelings of characters in both situations and tell how they would wish to be treated under similar circumstances. When the opportunity arises, remember to compliment the good sports in your classroom—on the playground, during your class spellathon—and encourage both the "Prunellas" and "Arthurs" on your teams!

Quiet Places to Study: Discussing Good Study Habits

Arthur spent a lot of time looking for quiet places to study his spelling words. Not all of us are fortunate enough to have a backyard treehouse like Arthur or the weather to accommodate such outdoor studying. Shortly after beginning our weekly spelling lists, we talk about the importance of having a quiet place to study away from the distractions of younger brothers and sisters, rambunctious pets, and blaring television sets.

I take a few minutes to have students tell where they usually practice their spelling words at home. We make a list of everything from the kitchen table, a quiet corner with a pillow, a bed or desk in a bedroom, or a coffee table in the living room. We talk about problems they have when studying and together we generate possible solutions to make studying at home more productive.

I invite students to bring in photos from home showing them studying spelling words in "quiet places." We display the photos on a poster of "Our Quiet Places to Study."

What Dictionary Are You Using?: Sharpening Dictionary Skills

During the spellathon, the Brain asked the principal what dictionary he was using to spell the word *fear*. To illustrate this point, I grab two or three dictionaries and look up the word *fear* with the students. Together we check the spelling and read the definitions and conclude that no matter which dictionary you refer to, the spelling and meaning of words will be the same.

Using words from *Arthur's Teacher Trouble* such as *principal, microphone, exclaimed, strictest, represent, gulped,* and *whispered,* we do a little work to sharpen our dictionary skills. If possible, give a dictionary to each team of partners. Students first estimate whether a particular word will be found in the beginning, middle, or end of the dictionary (some beginning dictionaries are color-coded for this purpose). We practice using guide words for help in locating words then discuss the different parts of each entry such as phonetic and conventional spellings, definitions, endings for the word, and sample sentences using each word.

This discussion often serves as an introduction to a Dictionary Skills Center. At this center students look up words in

Work from the Dictionary Skills Center

Sharpening Dictionary Skills

791

I think the word will be found in the beginning, middle, or end of the dictionary.

Book spelling of word: Preparation.

Sound spelling of word: Preperashen.

Possible endings for word: preparation's.

Here is a definition of the word: to prepare for something.

Here is the word used in a sentence: the knights got prepared for the war.

one of the dictionaries provided and then record information such as a short
definition, the page number where a word was found, guide words, or a
sample sentence. Copies of the form below will assist students when
recording this information independently at the Dictionary Skills Center.

*Practice Sheet
Used at the
Dictionary
Skills Center* ▷

☆ ✩ ☆ Sharpening Dictionary Skills ✩ ☆ ✩

I think the word will be found in the **beginning**, **middle**, or **end** of the dictionary.

Book spelling of word: _____

Sound spelling of word: _____

Possible endings for word: _____

Here is a definition of the word: _____

_____

Here is the word used in a sentence: _____

_____

Words in Our Memory Banks:
Making Personal Dictionaries

Let students see their progress! After weekly spelling tests have been graded
and returned to students, have them copy the words into Memory Bank
Booklets. Students label pages in a composition book from A to Z then
write words they can "book-spell" that begin with 'A' on the 'A' page, all
words that begin with 'B' on the 'B' page, and so on. As the number of
words in the booklets grows, so will students' confidence in their spelling
abilities. These handy references, like "real" dictionaries, reinforce editing
during writers' workshop and help students make the transition from sound-
spelling to conventional spelling.

To further reinforce dictionary skills, ask students to record entries in
their Memory Bank Booklet as they would appear in a dictionary with
sound spelling, book spelling, and an example of the word used in a
sentence. Since many words used as primary spelling words (i.e. *there* or
their) would be difficult for young children to define, this part of the
dictionary entry can be optional. Memory Bank Booklets make a great
companion to the Dictionary Skills Center described above.

How Much Is 100?: Estimating Items to 100

Gather 100 words, 100 pencils, 100 paper clips—100 of any item found in your classroom that will fit into a group for display. As students arrive one morning, give them a sheet of paper for recording their names 100 times. Or, provide paper plates for collecting 100 items from your math counting collections (blocks, paper clips, Unifix cubes, etc.). Take time for students to share their findings by comparing and contrasting the different ways 100 can be represented. This activity is fun to do on the 100th day of school.

Arthur's House: Making Details Count

When I notice it's time to encourage my students to add more detail to their writers' workshop illustrations, I bring *Arthur's Teacher Trouble* to a mini-lesson and focus their attention on two of my favorite illustrations of rooms inside Arthur's house. I hold up pages 8 and 9 to initiate a discussion of the items included in Arthur's kitchen. We marvel at how such details make us feel like we have gone home with Arthur after school and are sitting in his cozy kitchen, waiting for a snack.

I turn the page and we enter Arthur's bedroom where he works on a map of Africa. The students notice the bowl that matches the pitcher in his kitchen. We see a blue matching stripe pattern on Arthur's bedspread and curtains. His shelves are filled with toys and books. Stuffed animals and other toys crowd every available space. After speculating that Marc Brown may have received his inspiration from his sons' bedrooms and his own kitchen, I send the students to their seats with just one plain sheet of white paper, and Marc Brown's illustrations fresh in their minds. Their task is to fill in as much white space as possible by illustrating one of the rooms in their house. This illustration will serve as the beginning of a story for writers' workshop the next day. Combined with the book cover activity below, students have a chance to borrow illustrating techniques from a very creative Marc Brown—and learn about the importance of details in both art and writing.

Hannah's Bedroom

Marc Brown's Borders: Reviewing Patterns

Another illustrating trademark of Marc Brown is the way he uses borders to enhance his book covers and title pages. The alphabet border on the cover of *Arthur's Teacher Trouble* relates to the spelling theme of this book while the candy border on the title page of *Arthur's Birthday* reminds readers of treats at a birthday party. The pencils and crayons bordering the cover of *Arthur Writes a Story* are perfect for a book about story writing.

To further encourage details in illustrations and to review patterns from math, I make border patterns the focus of a mini-lesson. Together we chart these pattern ideas with a few of our own and then design book covers for the stories written in the activity "Arthur's House." I usually request that students include a particular number of steps (such as a three- or four-step pattern) in each border as an added challenge.

Student Book Cover with a Border
Inspired by Marc Brown ▶

More Books by Marc Brown

Arthur Babysits (Little, Brown and Company, 1992)

Arthur's Birthday (Little, Brown and Company, 1989)

Arthur's Computer Disaster (Little, Brown and Company, 1997)

Arthur's First Sleepover (Little, Brown and Company, 1994)

Arthur's Halloween (Little, Brown and Company, 1982)

Arthur's Perfect Christmas (Little, Brown and Company, 2000)

Arthur's Pet Business (Little, Brown and Company, 1990)

Arthur's Puppy (Little, Brown and Company, 1993)

Arthur's TV Trouble (Little, Brown and Company, 1995)

Arthur Writes a Story (Little, Brown and Company, 1996)

Arthur's Underwear (Little, Brown and Company, 1999)

Name _____ Date _____

Spelling Tricks and Tips

 **Tip #1** ## How to learn a new word

1. Look at the new word carefully while holding your breath.
2. Say the word 5 times as you jump up and down on one foot.
3. Spell the new word out loud, pointing to each letter in the word.
4. Close your eyes and picture the letters in the word.
5. Cover the word with a polka dot cloth then spell the word without looking.
6. Remove the cloth and spell the word again.

☆ **Repeat steps 1–6 five times for each word on your list.** ☆

 **Tip #2** ## Use spelling clues

1. Look and listen for little words inside the whole word (<u>fall</u>).
2. Rhyming words make spelling easier (<u>book</u>, <u>look</u>, <u>nook</u>, <u>shook</u>, <u>cook</u>, <u>hook</u>, <u>took</u>)
3. Know the vowel sounds—<u>a</u>, <u>e</u>, <u>i</u>, <u>o</u>, <u>u</u>—there is a vowel in every word.
4. Break long words into smaller parts—(Sep/tem/ber).
5. Some words you just have to look at and remember…(<u>friend</u> and <u>school</u>)

 **Tip #3** ## Preparing for the day of the test

1. Practice your words at home each night.
2. Get a good night's sleep the night before the test.
3. Eat a good breakfast on the morning of the test.
4. Just before the test, spin around 3 times while saying "I will take my time and spell my words carefully."

We are learning "Book Spelling!"

Dear Parents,

Today my class talked about the importance of using "book spelling"—spelling words as they appear in books. You might think of this as conventional spelling. Although we will continue to use sound spelling for writers' workshop and many other projects, we will be using book spelling for words that have been a part of our weekly spelling lists.

We read <u>Arthur's Teacher Trouble</u> by Marc Brown. The teacher, Mr. Ratburn, gave Arthur's class 100 words for their first spelling test. Luckily, our spelling list will only have 10–12 words, which we will get at the beginning of each week. We will practice in school every day and then have a test each Friday.

Arthur's friend Francine had a book of spelling tricks and tips. In this book we found a fun way to practice our words (breath holding, jumping up and down, and polka-dotted cloths are optional). We can do this at home together to practice new words. Here's how it works:

How to learn a new word:

1. Look at the new word carefully while holding your breath.
2. Say the word 5 times as you jump up and down on one foot.
3. Spell the new word out loud, pointing to each letter in the word.
4. Close your eyes and picture the letters in the word.
5. Cover the word with a polka dot cloth then spell the word without looking.
6. Remove the cloth and spell the word again.

☆ **Repeat steps 1–6 five times for each word on your list.** ☆

We also learned a few clues to help us spell words correctly. Here are the clues we talked about today:

1. Look and listen for little words inside the whole word (<u>fall</u>).
2. Rhyming words make spelling easier (<u>book</u>, <u>look</u>, <u>nook</u>, <u>shook</u>, <u>cook</u>, <u>hook</u>, <u>took</u>)
3. Know the vowel sounds—<u>a</u>, <u>e</u>, <u>i</u>, <u>o</u>, <u>u</u>—there is a vowel in every word.
4. Break long words into smaller parts—(Sep/tem/ber).
5. Some words you just have to look at and remember…(<u>friend</u> and <u>school</u>)

Please help me practice the words on my list for 10–15 minutes each night. Then help me make sure to get a good night's rest and a nutritious breakfast before my test on Friday.

Thanks,
your child ♡

Chapter Five

I Think I'll Move to Australia

LESSONS 41 TO 50

Alexander and the Terrible, Horrible, No Good, Very Bad Day
by Judith Viorst

Mini-Lessons Across the Curriculum

Language Arts

Greetings from Alexander	*Reviewing words that end in silent 'e'*
Letters to Alexander	*Practicing spelling words with silent 'e'*
Silent 'e'—A.K.A. Bossy *E*	*Charting more words with silent 'e'*
Terrible, Horrible, No Good, Very Bad	*Exploring synonyms*
Alexander's Perfectly Wonderful, So Good, Never Bad Day	*Writing more Alexander stories*

Math & Science

Developing Concepts of Time	*Minutes and hours*
Cereal Box Prizes	*Thinking about probability*
Favorite Desserts	*Graphing student choices*

Community

Alexander Takes Control	*Making a T-Chart of Alexander's Day*
Patching Things Up	*Role-playing conflict resolution*

Greetings from Alexander

GOAL *Reviewing Words That End in Silent 'e'*

> I went to sleep with gum in my mouth and now there's gum in my hair and when I got out of bed this morning I tripped on the skateboard and by mistake I dropped my sweater in the sink while the water was running and I could tell it was going to be a terrible, horrible, no good, very bad day.
>
> ~*Alexander and the Terrible, Horrible, No Good, Very Bad Day* by Judith Viorst, pp. 5.

lexander and the Terrible, Horrible, No Good, Very Bad Day is a book for the bookshelf of every primary classroom. Written in 1972, this may be one of the first books written to help young children appreciate the importance of not sweating the small stuff. Alexander's day begins with such problems as having no prize in his breakfast cereal and getting scrunched in the car pool and ends with having a burned out night light at bedtime, making Alexander wish he could move to Australia.

While young children relate to his feelings of anger and frustration, they take comfort in knowing that everyone has "those days" occasionally. Many often admit to having said unpleasant things to friends, to having punched a sibling instead of using words to settle a disagreement, to having felt like running away rather than dealing with a problem. Seeing a favorite book character react similarly to problems allows for a great discussion of how best to handle these problems when facing them in our own lives.

After reading and discussing *Alexander and the Terrible, Horrible, No Good, Very Bad Day* for read aloud, I bring this book to a word study lesson in which Alexander writes a letter to the class. In the letter Alexander talks about his day before falling asleep with a more positive outlook on tomorrow. Since it is time for a study of silent 'e' words, the letter is conveniently written with lots of these words but, in the letter, the silent 'e' is missing.

Inviting a favorite book character like Alexander to the lesson adds more excitement to the usual study of silent 'e' words and makes studying the words more meaningful since the words were written by Alexander for a purpose, not written and studied in isolation.

I copy the following letter on the board, distribute individual chalkboards and chalk to students and we are ready for a mini-lesson based on *Alexander and the Terrible, Horrible, No Good, Very Bad Day.*

September 22

Dear Friends,

I hop you can read this because I am writing it with my flashlight for light. My Micky Mouse night light burned out. Just one of many things that mad today a terrible, horrible, no good, very bad day! My mom tells me some days are lik that even in Australia which is where I think I'll move if I have another day lik today. My mom tells me to think of something that maks me smil —Lik riding my bik on the trails or taking a hik in the woods. But then I see myself wearing plain whit sneakers instead of blu ones with red strips and I get mad all over again. I can think about the piece of cak Mom promised to pack in my lunch tomorrow but then I think of Dr. Fields fixing my cavity next week. It was a terrible, horrible, no good, very bad day but I guess when you think about it, tomorrow has to be better! Maybe I won't have to move to Australia after all.

Sincerely,

Alexander

Mrs. L.: Alexander has written a letter to us.

Ben: I see a mistake that he made.

Eric: So do I.

Mrs. L.: It does look like he misspelled a few words. Let's try to read the letter to find out what Alexander is telling us. Then you can help me fix the mistakes.

Hannah: Alexander probably doesn't want to know he's having spelling problems, too.

Mrs. L.:	Maybe we can help him become a better speller. You can read the letter silently while I point to the words in Alexander's letter. Remember to raise your hand if you come to a word you don't know and I'll say that word out loud for you. Let's read to find out if Alexander is feeling better after his terrible…
Class:	Horrible, no good, very bad day…

The students read the letter silently as I read the letter out loud. First we discuss the content of the letter. Then I begin a discussion on our word study focus: silent 'e.'

Mrs. L.:	Tell me why Alexander thought we might have a problem reading this letter.
Tyler:	Because he didn't have a light except his flashlight. His Mickey Mouse night light burned out.
Collin:	I had a hard time reading the letter because some of the words didn't look right. I've never seen *hik* or *bik* before.
Molly:	Alexander forgot to put the *e* on the end of the words. They should be h-i-k-e and b-i-k-e.
Mrs. L.:	You're right, Molly. Would you please come up and put the silent 'e' on the end of these words and then we'll start at the beginning of the letter and fix Alexander's other mistakes. He did a wonderful job of writing the letter except for words with silent 'e.'
Madison:	But he used good sound spelling.
Mrs. L.:	Yes, he did. What is the job of silent 'e' in words?
Lauren:	It makes the other letter in the word say its name.
Tori:	The other vowel says its name.
Mrs. L.:	Exactly. So in the word *hike*, silent 'e''s job is—
Alex:	To make the *i* say its name.
Mrs. L.:	Great. Without the silent 'e,' *hike* would have a short sound for *i* and the word would be—
Class:	Hik.
Matthew:	That doesn't make sense.
Mrs. L.:	Let's look at the first sentence to find other words that need a silent 'e.' Please read this sentence with me:
Class:	*I hop you can read this because I am writing it with only my flashlight for light.*
Mrs. L.:	Any words that need silent 'e'?
Hannah:	Yes, it should be *hope* not *hop*.
Mrs. L.:	I agree. Hannah, would you please add the *e* to *hop* while the rest of the class writes H-O-P-E on their chalkboards then circles the silent 'e.' Let's continue reading the letter out loud together. You say stop when you see a word that needs a silent 'e.' Then we'll stop to fix it.

We continue reading, stopping at and correcting words that are missing silent 'e.'

Helpful Tips for Using a Daily Letter with Your Class

☀ Read the entire letter out loud together and briefly discuss the content.

☀ Reread each sentence prior to having students search for individual words.

☀ Use a pointer to help keep students focused when reading out loud or asking students to find particular words.

☀ Have volunteers circle words on the board as the rest of the class copies words onto a lap-sized chalkboard or individual recording sheet.

☀ Always put the letter back together at the end of the lesson by reading the letter from beginning to end again. This helps students see the words you've isolated by a particular skill back in a meaningful context.

Mrs. L.: Nice work, boys and girls. Let's read the list of words on your chalkboards. Make sure you included the silent 'e' at the end of each word:

hope	smile	blue
made	bike	stripes
like III	hike	cake
make	white	

Mrs. L.: A few of these words are completely different words without the e—

Stephanie: Like *hop*,

Sam: *Strip*

Lauren: And *mad*.

Mrs. L.: When you add the silent 'e,' *hop* becomes—

Class: *Hope*.

Mrs. L.: *Strip* becomes—

Class: *Stripe*.

Mrs. L.: And *mad* becomes—

Class: *Made*.

Tori: Words like *bik* and *hik* just don't make sense without the *e*.

Hannah: *Bik* and *hik* are just nonsense words.

Mrs. L.: Once you know that certain words contain silent 'e,' usually their rhyming word pairs have silent 'e,' too.

Matthew: Like *bike* and *hike*—

Elizabeth: And *like*!

Mrs. L.: Right! Can you think of any other words that would have silent 'e' when you write them in book spelling—words that rhyme with silent 'e' words from Alexander's letter?

Courtney: *Rope* rhymes with *hope* so it would be r-o-p-e.

Mrs. L.: Great!

David: *Nope*.

Alex: *Mope*.

Mrs. L.: Great words!

Emma: *Rake* would be spelled r-a-k-e like *make* and *cake*.

Mrs. L.: You're right. There is a silent 'e' word in Alexander's letter with an -i-n-g ending whose root word rhymes with *make* and *cake*. Do you see a word with -i-n-g?

David: But *write* doesn't rhyme with *make* and *cake*.

Stephanie: *Taking*! Take off the -i-n-g and you have *take*.

Tyler: But there isn't an *e* on the end.

Mrs. L.: When you write the word *take*, it's spelled t-a-k-e. The *e* gets dropped before you add the -i-n-g ending. The word *write* follows the same rule. The silent 'e' drops off before the -i-n-g is added. So *write* is spelled w-r-i-t-e. There's one more word like this in Alexander's letter...

Samantha: *Riding.* It has a long *i* sound so it could end in silent 'e.'

Mrs. L.: *Ride* is spelled—

Class: R-i-d-e.

Mrs. L.: You're right. Any other words with -i-n-g?

Ben: *Fixing.* But that doesn't have a long vowel sound. *Fix* is spelled f-i-x.

Mrs. L.: Nice work with words, boys and girls. Now it's your turn to practice writing some silent 'e' words of your own.

Independent Practice

Letters to Alexander: Practicing Spelling Words with Silent 'e'

Mrs. L.: I thought it might be nice for you to write a letter to Alexander.

Eric: To cheer him up.

Mrs. L.: Sure. To let him know you hope tomorrow is a better day than his terrible, horrible, no good, very bad day.

Collin: And to find out if his mother really packed the piece of cake in his lunch.

Mrs. L.: You could ask him about that. You could also tell Alexander about a terrible, horrible, no good, very bad day of your own. And—most importantly—what you did to cheer up on your terrible, horrible day.

Lauren: It might make him feel better if he knows we've had bad days, too.

Mrs. L.: Exactly. As you're writing, think about words that might need a silent 'e'. Especially words that rhyme with other silent 'e' words from Alexander's letter. Circle the silent 'e' words in your letter to show Alexander which words have silent 'e' in them.

David: This would be a nice hint to Alexander about silent 'e' words so that the next time he writes a letter to us, it's easier to read.

As the boys and girls head back to their seats to write an encouraging letter to Alexander, I'm thinking about Alexander's next letter to us.

Writing Letters to Alexander ▶

8 More Book-Based Lessons

Silent 'e', A.K.A. Bossy E: Charting More Words with Silent 'e'

Thanks to a little boy in my class a few years ago, silent 'e' has affectionately become known as "Bossy *E*" (see my *Literature Based Mini-Lessons to Teach Decoding and Word Recognition*, Scholastic Professional Books, 2000). After explaining that the job of silent 'e' is to tell the other vowel in the word to say its name, this student commented that silent 'e' sounds more like a "Bossy *E*" to him! I decided that this year, it might be fun to have Alexander share another letter with the class, this time talking about "Bossy *E*."

After reading the following letter, we make a chart of "Words that Follow Bossy *E*'s Rule" and begin by recording those words from Alexander's letter that have Bossy *E*. As the students quickly learn, the so-called rules in our language are often broken. So we add another chart—"Words that Break Bossy *E*'s Rule." On this chart, we record words with Bossy *E* but whose other vowels do not say their name. The charts become handy references during writing time as the list grows to include other Bossy *E* words we encounter, as well. These charts and our discussions about words help students develop an awareness of the many words that end in Bossy *E*— whether the other vowel says its name or not!

Dear Friends,

Thanks for the letters. They made me feel better. It's nice to know that other kids sometimes have bad days, too. Today my only problem was having my cavity filled and even that wasn't so terribly horrible.

My class has been learning about Bossy E. Bossy E is an e at the end of a word and has the job to tell the other vowel in the word to say its name. I'm getting better at writing these words with book spelling but could use a little practice. Maybe you could make a list of words that follow this rule for me.

Thanks,
Alexander

P.S. My mom did remember to give me cake in my lunch. It was chocolate cake with peanut butter icing.

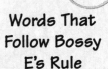

Words That Follow Bossy E's Rule

rule	name
made	these
nice	cake
time	make

Words That Break Bossy E's Rule

terrible	little
horrible	chocolate
practice	have

Terrible, Horrible, No Good, Very Bad: Exploring Synonyms

Take the opportunity to introduce synonyms with the book *Alexander and the Terrible, Horrible, No Good, Very Bad Day*. In this story, reusing the words "terrible, horrible, no good, very bad" along with "I think I'll move to Australia," becomes predictable and fun, as Alexander repeats them each time he faces yet another challenging event. Explain that this story is an exception—in most instances, using the same old tired words in a story is boring.

Demonstrate to the class how a writer uses a thesaurus to replace tired words with synonyms. Begin by looking up *terrible* in the thesaurus and sharing the other options for this word. Along with *horrible*, the words *awful, unpleasant, dreadful, horrendous, shocking, frightful, ugly*, and *appalling* are offered as replacements for *terrible*. To further expand students' vocabularies, help them remember options for overused words, and to provide a reference for future use, make student thesauruses.

First make copies of page 82. Cut the pages in half and staple together into booklets. Have students write a "tired" word in the first blank and work with a partner to come up with one or more synonyms for the given word. You may wish to have students use a thesaurus for locating synonyms or have students brainstorm options of their own. Finally, have students write a sentence that replaces the tired word with two other optional words. If the synonym is used appropriately, the meaning of the sentence will not be changed and the sentence will still make sense.

In the sample below, we wrote a sentence together using three replacements or synonyms for *terrible*.

> When I'm tired of using the word terrible, I can replace it with the word awful, or unpleasant, or horrendous.

Here is an example of the same sentence using synonyms for this tired word:

☼ The birthday cake tasted terrible because Mother forgot to add the sugar.

☼ The birthday cake tasted awful because Mother forgot to add the sugar.

☼ The birthday cake tasted horrendous because Mother forgot to add the sugar.

(For more lessons on synonyms, see *Literature Based Mini-Lessons to Teach Writing*, Scholastic Professional Books, 1998.)

Developing Concepts of Time: Minutes and Hours

Twenty-four hours most likely felt like forever to Alexander on his terrible, horrible, no good, very bad day. The following intervals of time give students an introduction to the concept of one minute and one hour.

First, have students face you with their backs to the classroom clock. After you say "go" to begin timing, students raise a hand whenever they think one minute is up. Many students will be surprised to hear you say "stop" at the end of this 60 seconds, well before or after they have raised their hands. Be sure to repeat this activity several times to help students become familiar with one minute of time. Next, give intervals of two minutes and three minutes a try. Since students usually sit very quietly counting the minutes away, this is a great activity when your students need a quiet break.

For another lesson in how time flies, try the following activity to help students develop a sense of one hour of time. First, use "The Hours in Our Day" reproducible found on page 83 to make a blank chart similar to the sample shown on this page. Beginning at 9:00, for example, record what you are doing then announce that you will set a timer to go off in one hour. When it rings, pause in your routine to record what you were doing at 10:00. Reset the timer to go off at the top of each new hour throughout the school day. If the class is at lunch or out to recess when the timer rings, simply adjust the timer and record what you were doing when it went off. (If you went to lunch from 11:50–12:20, for example, record lunch for 12:00 then set your timer to go off at 1:00.) For extra practice, ask students to use a timer and recording sheet at home to record their routine upon arriving home from school to bedtime.

Charting the Hours in Our Day ▶

The Hours of Our Day

At 9:00 we have our Opening Routine

At 10:00 we have Writers' Workshop

At 11:00 we have Book Time

Cereal Box Prizes: Thinking About Probability

Most students agree the probability that Alexander would wake up with gum in his hair is high given the fact that he went to bed with gum in his mouth. But a prize-less breakfast cereal box seems unlikely and most unfair—especially since Anthony found a Corvette Sting Ray car kit in his cereal and Nick found a Junior Undercover Agent code ring in his. Engage students in a lesson on probability based on a new box of wheat pops for Alexander.

Give each student a copy of Alexander's new box of cereal (page 84) then read the guarantee which claims "A prize in every box." The question for students to ponder is whether this box will have a Free Toy Coupon, an Invisible Ink Pen, or be another prize-less box. Have students imagine a mechanical prize machine that randomly selects the prize from a pile of four Free Toy Coupons, two Invisible Ink Pens, and one Sorry No Prize.

Give students a chance to do a probability test using the pictures of the cereal box prizes as manipulatives. After making a prediction about what prize will most likely be in Alexander's box of Wheat Pops, students cut apart the pictures of the prizes and place them in a paper bag. After giving the bag a shake, students pick a prize from the bag and record it on the chart. Students repeat this procedure nine more times for a total of ten selections. After all prizes have been picked, discuss results then answer the remaining statement on the paper. This lesson on probability can have some surprising results!

Cereal Box Prizes

Alexander Takes Control: Making a T-Chart of Alexander's Day

It's a true that "some days are like that"—even in Australia. It's also true that some of Alexander's problems could have been prevented. Helping students understand that they do have some control over the events in their lives is an important realization that can help them make different choices in their day-to-day interactions with others.

Using *Alexander and the Terrible, Horrible, No Good, Very Bad Day*, we make a T-Chart of the events of his day, listing those things in his control on the left and those things that were out of his control on the right. We discuss each situation carefully using if-then statements. For example, if Alexander went to bed with gum in his mouth, there is a great chance he will wake up with gum in his hair. This is just one event in Alexander's horrible day that could have been prevented because it was in his control. Not getting a prize in his cereal box, however, was completely out of his control.

When students see the number of things that Alexander could have prevented by taking control, they begin to realize his day didn't have to be as terrible as it was. We relate Alexander's lack of control to situations that could have been prevented in our own lives—such as getting a time-out for hitting a sibling or forgetting a library book by not packing it in a backpack the night before. Our finished T-Chart looked something like this:

Alexander Could Control	Alexander Could Not Control
waking with gum in his hair	breakfast cereal prize
putting his skate board away	being by the window in the car
being careful with his sweater	Paul's unkind words to Alexander
drawing an invisible castle	no dessert in his lunch
skipping number 16	falling in the mud
singing too loud	plain white sneakers
saying unkind words to Paul	lima beans for dinner
getting a cavity	railroad train pajamas
elevator door on his foot	Nick taking pillow back
punching Nick	cat sleeping with Anthony
playing with Dad's copying machine	biting tongue
playing with Dad's phone	Mickey Mouse night light burned out
kissing on TV (turn TV off)	
bath too hot (test it before getting in)	
soap in eyes (be careful)	

Language Arts

Alexander's Perfectly Wonderful, So Good, Never Bad Day: Writing More Alexander Stories

Using the ideas listed on the T-Chart from the "Alexander Takes Control" activity, I ask students to help me write a new story beginning for a book titled "Alexander's Terrific, Wonderful, So Good, Never Bad Day." As a class, we rewrite the first sentence using the text of *Alexander's Terrible, Horrible, No Good, Very Bad Day* as a guide:

> I went to sleep and dreamed a great dream. I woke up to hear birds singing and my cat purring at the foot of my bed. In my cereal box was an instant prize coupon to buy any toy at the toy store. I could tell it was going to be a perfectly wonderful, so good, never bad day.

The students and I do our best to turn Alexander's terrible, horrible, no good, very bad day into a story about a day that is just the opposite. We brainstorm a list of these opposites as main ideas. You may wish to rewrite the entire story for a language experience lesson over the course of several writers' workshop periods. To make the story more fun, we make the wonderful things that happen a bit outlandish, as well. For example, while sitting in the seat next to the window in the car pool, Alexander spots a diamond ring on the sidewalk and receives a reward from the owner. His powerful singing voice lands him the lead in the spring musical production and Alexander gets three desserts in his lunch box since his mother made a mistake and put Anthony's and Nick's in his lunch box along with his own.

For writers' workshop, students then write their own versions of similarly wonderful days. A segment from "Emma's Terrific, Wonderful, So Good, Never Bad Day" is featured below.

A "Wonderful Day" Story. ▶

When I woke up my room was clean and my cat was at the bottom of my bed. When I went downstairs there was two blueberry mufins on the table in my spot. When I went out to play I was up to bat.

Favorite Desserts:
Graphing Student Choices

Two cupcakes, a Hershey bar with almonds, or a jelly roll with coconut sprinkles? What would you most hope to find in your lunch as a special dessert? I write this question on a sheet of construction paper along with pictures of the three dessert options. Under each picture, I make a small hole using a paper punch. I display this "graph" on the front board for my students to think about as they arrive one morning. I give each student a Learning Link to attach in a chain under their dessert choice picture. I save my vote for a Hershey Bar with almonds for last.

This quick and easy graph serves as a kick-off to our math lesson that afternoon. As we discuss the results of our graph, I discover why two cupcakes is the favorite dessert of our class—*Two* cupcakes is more of a treat than one jelly roll or chocolate bar.

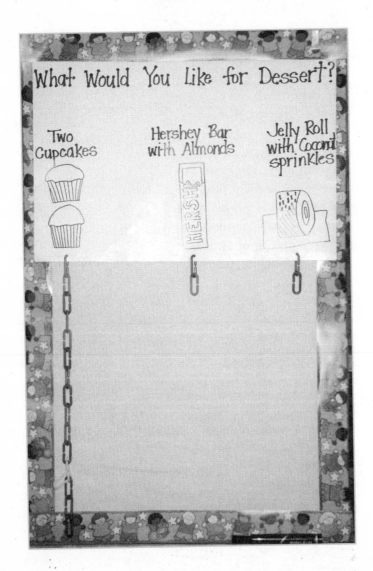

Our Favorite Desserts Graph

Patching Things Up:
Role-Playing Conflict Resolution

Relationships can be in a constant state of flux among first and second graders. Best friend, second best friend, and third best friend status can change from one recess to the next. Helping students express their feelings, understand the feelings of another, and solve matters before they escalate is a valuable life skill worth practicing.

Use Alexander's problem with Paul (pages 12–13 of *Alexander and the Terrible, Horrible, No Good, Very Bad Day*) to set the stage for some role-playing. Begin the role-play with two students playing the parts of Alexander and Paul. Paul announces that Alexander has been demoted to third best friend status behind Philip Parker and Albert Moyo. Alexander says to Paul, "I hope you sit on a tack. I hope the next time you get a double-decker strawberry ice-cream cone the ice cream part falls off the cone part and lands in Australia."

What are the next words spoken? Choose another student to play the part of a friend who intervenes with some words of assistance. After offering several possible solutions to the problem, we role-play more appropriate ways for Alexander to have handled this problem in the first place.

More Books by Judith Viorst

Alexander—Who's Not (Do You Hear Me? I Mean It) Going to Move (Atheneum Books for Young Readers, 1995)

Alexander, Who Used to Be Rich Last Sunday (Aladdin Books, 1978)

Earrings (Atheneum Books, 1990)

I'll Fix Anthony (HarperCollins Publishers, 1969)

Rosie and Michael (Aladdin Books, 1974)

The Tenth Good Thing About Barney (Atheneum Books, 1971)

Synonyms

When I'm tired of using the word _____ ,

I can replace it with the word _____ ,

or _____ ,

or _____ .

Here is an example of the same sentence with synonyms for this tired word:

_____

_____

_____

Synonyms

When I'm tired of using the word _____ ,

I can replace it with the word _____ ,

or _____ ,

or _____ .

Here is an example of the same sentence with synonyms for this tired word:

_____

_____

_____

Name _____

Date _____

The Hours in Our Day

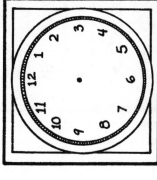

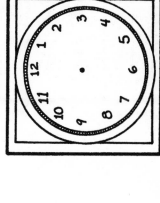

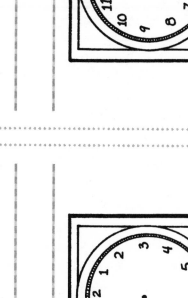

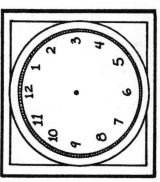

 Free Toy Coupon

 Free Toy Coupon

 Free Toy Coupon

 Free Toy Coupon

 Sorry! No Prize in this Box

Invisible Ink Pen

Invisible Ink Pen

Name _____

Date _____

Cereal Box Prizes

New and Improved
Wheat Pops!

A Prize in EVERY Box!

A Free Toy Coupon
Good at your favorite toy store!

or

An Invisible Ink Pen
For sending special agent messages

Directions: In this activity, you will predict which kind of coupon you are most likely to choose out of the ones pictured on the right. Record your prediction in the space below.

I think I will pick the _____ most often.

Then follow these steps to test your prediction:

1. Color the coupons below; then cut them out.

2. Place them all in a paper bag. Hold the bag shut and shake it, mixing the coupons together.

3. Reach into the bag and take out one coupon.

4. Record the prize listed on the coupon on the recording sheet.

5. Put the coupon back in the bag.

Repeat this process 9 times. When you're finished, complete the sentences below. Was your prediction correct?

I picked the _____ most often.

In second place was the _____

and last was the _____ .

	Free Toy	Invisible Ink Pen	No Prize
①			
②			
③			
④			
⑤			
⑥			
⑦			
⑧			
⑨			
⑩			

Chapter Six

My Own Sixty-Four Crayola Crayons

LESSONS 51 TO 60

The Art Lesson
by Tomie dePaola

Mini-Lessons Across the Curriculum

Language Arts

Sixty-Four Crayola Crayons	***Writing analogies to describe colors***
Our Own Crayon Analogies	*Practicing analogies*
When I Grow Up	*Writing keepsake stories*
Doing Favorite Things	*Identifying verbs as action words*
Practice, Practice, Practice!	*Using analogies to describe feelings*
Favorite Parts	*Discussing literature*

Math & Science

Crayola Math	*Using crayons as manipulatives for multiplication*

Art

No More Painting on the Walls	*Painting murals of school activities*
Primary Colors	*Exploring how colors are made*
Another Art Lesson	*Borrowing illustration techniques*

Sixty-Four Crayola Crayons

GOAL *Writing Analogies to Describe Colors*

> ❝ Tommy could hardly wait. He practiced all summer. Then, on his birthday, which was right after school began, his mom and dad gave him a box of sixty-four Crayola Crayons. Regular boxes of crayons had red, orange, yellow, green, blue, violet, brown and black. This box had so many other colors: blue-violet, turquoise, red-orange, pink and even gold, silver and copper. ❞
>
> ~*The Art Lesson* by Tomie dePaola,
> pp. 20.

I n his memoir, Tomie dePaola writes of the greatly anticipated art lesson with Mrs. Bowers, the teacher who allowed him to express his love of art—by giving him another piece of paper and permitting him to use his own "birthday crayons," not school crayons. Although I don't tell students this story is based on real-life events, not long into the read aloud, someone always surmises that Tommy in *The Art Lesson* is really Tomie dePaola. As one student exclaimed, "That means he knew all the way back in first grade what he was really going to be when he grew up!"

The writing mini-lesson that follows our read-aloud shows students how to use analogies in writing to make the stories they write more exciting. Using a box of 64 Crayola crayons with such colors as asparagus green, robin's egg blue, carnation pink, and dandelion yellow has students painting—or in this case coloring—pictures with words in no time at all.

The impact of the lesson lies in the images the analogies make for young writers as well as the simplicity of this writing technique. To write with analogies, all students need to remember is *as* _____ *as*

_____ to turn a pair of *blue eyes* into *eyes as blue as a robin egg*. So grab a box of 64 Crayola Crayons—wrapped in birthday paper, if you like—make copies of page 96, and meet students for a fun and easy writers'-workshop mini-lesson that will give students a simple yet effective writing technique for "coloring" pictures with words.

Teaching Tip

Write student names on individual popsicle sticks then place in a small basket or paper-covered juice can. When it's time to choose a student to help with a special task, such as opening a present in this lesson, shake the basket, pick a stick and your helper has been chosen fairly.

Mrs. L.:	I brought a present to share with you today. Would you like to help me open it?
Eric:	I will…It's a box of crayons.
Mrs. L.:	Not just any box of crayons. It's a box of 64 Crayola Crayons.
Elizabeth:	Just like in the book *The Art Lesson*.
Mrs. L.:	You're right! I thought it might be fun to use these crayons for our writers' workshop mini-lesson. A box of crayons like this was special to Tommy.
Emma:	He liked the many different colors like copper and silver.
Mrs. L.:	Right. School crayons don't have these colors, do they?
Ben:	No, just the usual colors: red, green, blue, purple and others like that.
Madison:	Boxes of 64 Crayola crayons have better names for the colors, too—like hot pink and fuchsia.
Tori:	They need fancier names because there's more than one color of blue in the box so each crayon has to have a different name.
David:	I like the way they write the names on all the crayons.
Lauren:	I think it would be fun to be the one who gets to invent the names on crayons.
Mrs. L.:	Me, too. In fact, today I thought it might be fun to use our new box of 64 Crayola crayons to help us with our writers' workshop mini-lesson. We'll use these new crayons to help us write some analogies.
Tyler:	Some what?
Mrs. L.:	Analogies. Making analogies is a way to paint pictures with words. They are an easy and fun way to make the words in your story more exciting. To write with analogies, you need to remember this:

as _____ as _____

I take a crayon from the box.

Jack:	You chose a green one.
Mrs. L.:	Not just a green crayon but a shade of green that is as green as asparagus. Asparagus is the name of this crayon.
Elizabeth:	Asparagus is my mom's favorite vegetable. It is green like that.
Mrs. L.:	Yes, it is. And when you think of all the shades of green there are, knowing something is as green as asparagus paints a clear picture in your mind of this exact shade. I will write *as green as asparagus* on the board for our first analogy. I'll use the asparagus crayon to color a circle beside this analogy to illustrate this color.

Samantha:	Plain green is in the box, too.
Mrs. L.:	You're right. In my box, the regular crayons, as Tomie called them, are all in the first section of the box. Here's what plain green looks like.
Lauren:	There are a lot of other colors of green in the box, too.
Mrs. L.:	You're right. Let's take a look at a few other shades of green. Sam, would you pick one please?
Sam:	Here's sea green.
Mrs. L.:	Let's make an analogy for this color—
Sam:	It's probably named sea green because it looks as green as the sea.
Mrs. L.:	The green of the sea is different from the green of asparagus, isn't it? As a writer, it would help to describe the shade of green using an analogy. Analogies like *as green as asparagus* or *as green as the sea* help writers paint pictures with words. Let's choose another shade of green from the box to see what other analogies we can use to help us paint pictures with words.
Courtney:	Here's spring green. That's a light shade of green.
Mrs. L.:	Tell me why you think this is called spring green.
Courtney:	It's a kind of green you see only in the spring?
David:	When the leaves first pop open after winter.
Matthew:	Sometimes those leaves look more light green than dark green.
Mrs. L.:	So an analogy for this color would be as green as...
Class:	*Spring!*
Stephanie:	Or as green as leaves in the spring.
Madison:	That sounds better!
Mrs. L.:	I agree. You get a more detailed picture of spring. Who would like to choose another crayon?
Eric:	It says *Granny Smith Apple.* I love Granny Smith apples!
Anna:	Me, too.
Mrs. L.:	What a clever way to describe this shade of green. As green as...
Class:	A Granny Smith apple.
Mrs. L.:	So if you wrote the words *as green as a Granny Smith apple* in one of your stories, you would want readers to picture this shade of green rather than one of these other shades.
Hannah:	My sweater is that color.
Mrs. L.:	Yes, it is. If a character in a writers' workshop story was wearing that sweater, the author could write, *she wore a sweater as green as a Granny Smith apple.* Looks like we have two green crayons left to choose.
Elizabeth:	This one is yellow green.
Mrs. L.:	Yes, it is. Tyler, would you choose the last green crayon?
Tyler:	Green yellow.
Mrs. L.:	Tell me about these last two colors.
Tyler:	The yellow green looks more yellow than green and the green yellow looks more green than yellow.

Elizabeth: I think they ran out of analogy words for this one.

Mrs. L.: It sounds like you prefer the colors that are described using things you can picture like apples and spring, olives and asparagus.

Class: Yes!

Mrs. L.: I feel the same way when I read a story. When words paint pictures, the story is much more memorable. Let's pick a few more colors before writing some analogies of our own.

We choose and discuss five or six more colors.

Mrs. L.: Now let's read our list of analogies. [See list at right.]

Now it's time for you to create some of your own crayon names. All you need is your "school" crayons, your imagination, your new understanding of analogies, and a crayon recording sheet.

Crayon Analogies

as green as asparagus
as green as the sea
as green as leaves in spring
as green as an olive
as green as the forest
as green as a Granny Smith apple
as orange as macaroni and cheese
as pink as your cheeks when you're being tickled
as pink as a carnation
as yellow as a dandelion
as blue as a robin's egg
as blue as the Pacific Ocean
as red as a brick
as red as a wild strawberry
as purple as a plum
as purple as a distant majestic mountain

Independent Practice

Our Own Crayon Analogies: Practicing Analogies

I send students to their seats with a Crayon Recording Sheet (page 96). Their job is to choose five crayons from their own boxes of 16 crayons and think of a new name for each color using an analogy. Students write the analogies on the Crayon Recording Sheet. Finally, students choose a favorite analogy to be placed on a bulletin board titled '64 Crayola Crayons.' Extra copies of the crayon recording sheets are placed in a folder and hung near the bulletin board along with a box of 64 Crayola Crayons. During free time, students can rename other crayons as we attempt to create 64 different analogies for our bulletin board.

At right are a few of the students' favorite analogies that resulted from our independent practice time:

as red as Clifford
as green as a Christmas tree
as orange as a pumpkin
as purple as a grape
as brown as a chocolate Lab
as black as the night time sky
as yellow as corn on the cob
as white as a stick of gum

8 More Book-Based Lessons

When I Grow Up: Writing Keepsake Stories

"Tommy knew he wanted to be an artist when he grew up" begins Tomie dePaola's *The Art Lesson*. What do your students wish to be when they grow up? Give your aspiring young writers, teachers, doctors, architects, chefs, and scientists an outlet for recording their future plans. Discuss how it is possible to know career choices at an early age just like Tomie dePaola. Use *The Art Lesson* as a model for stories based on this theme of "when I grow up." To get students started, you may wish to copy the first sentence from *The Art Lesson* on the board as follows:

_____ knew (s)he wanted to be a _____ when (s)he grew up.

Ask students to complete the sentence in their own way. Encourage those who are unsure of their future career choices to think about what they like to do with their time. Tomie dePaola drew and drew and drew for fun. I used to play school each day using all my stuffed animals as students. Eric builds with Lego blocks for hours—does this mean he will be an architect?

Provide time for sharing these stories of future plans, making sure to discuss or add any analogies to paint pictures with words. Display these keepsake stories for Back to School Night or share during parent-teacher conferences. Who knows, there just may be a future Tomie dePaola in your class!

A Few Beginning Sentences from Our "When I Grow Up" Stories

Practice, Practice, Practice!: Using Analogies to Describe Feelings

In *The Art Lesson*, Tommy went from being as excited as a kid in a toy store—to as disappointed as a boy who lost his dog. Have your students practice writing more analogies, this time to describe feelings. Together, write analogies to describe how Tommy may have felt:

☀ on the day of his first art lesson.

☀ when he opened his box of birthday crayons.

☀ when Miss Landers told him to take his birthday crayons home.

☀ when Mrs. Bowers told him he could have another piece of paper.

Chart these and other analogies discovered in books and in students' writing. Discuss the popular saying "as happy as a clam" then provide students with copies of the "As Happy as a Clam" recording sheet found on page 97, as well. Attached to a writers' workshop folder these individual recording sheets will provide students with a handy reference that will in time reflect the many ways authors use analogies to paint pictures with words.

(For another mini-lesson on analogies, see *Literature Based Mini-Lessons to Teach Writing*, Scholastic, 1998).

Favorite Parts: Discussing Literature

At the beginning of the school year, when I ask my students what they like best about a particular book, the responses typically are "everything" or "the pictures." Providing students with opportunities to voice opinions and hear those expressed by others helps them better appreciate any given story.

To kick-off a discussion of favorite parts of Tomie dePaola's *The Art Lesson*, I share how my favorite part is discovering that this really is a true story about Tomie dePaola. I show the last page, where "Tommy," all grown up and shown with gray hair, is still drawing. I point out other details on this page that show—rather than tell—readers that this is a true story. For example, some of the pictures on the walls are from stories written and illustrated by Tomie dePaola as an adult. After hearing my favorite part, the students add ideas of their own. Their top three answers are typically:

☀ when Tommy gets to draw all over the walls of his new house

☀ when Tommy draws on his sheets

☀ when he sneaks his box of 64 Crayola Crayons to school

With each new discussion about literature, the students are better equipped to talk more specifically about favorite parts of books shared.

Primary Colors: Exploring How Colors Are Made

Give your students an art lesson that explores how different colors are made from just three colors of paint. Provide groups of students with small wooden sticks for stirring, one or more sheets of white paper, and three paint cups—one for each of the primary colors—red, blue, and yellow. If painting doesn't fit into your schedule, let students mix crayon colors in a similar fashion. You may wish to allow free exploration of colors or provide more structure to the lesson by writing a few color combinations on the board to guide students:

red + blue =   red + yellow =   blue + yellow =

After students have made green, purple, black, brown, and orange, allow time for experimenting to make a shade of sea green or asparagus green or macaroni and cheese orange, for example. Or, students could use their own crayon names from the independent follow-up lesson to label their paint color creations.

Bring students together for a discussion of colors made. Introduce the concept of primary versus secondary colors. If time allows, pass out another piece of paper so that students may paint a picture using their new paint colors.

Exploring Colors ▶

Crayola Math: Using Crayons as Manipulatives for Multiplication

Shortly after reading *The Art Lesson* with my class, I brought my box of 64 Crayola Crayons to a math lesson and discovered crayons make colorful and effective manipulatives for a multiplication facts lesson on factors of 64. I began by asking the class to tell me about the groups of crayons organized inside the box. The students are quick to see that there are 4 divisions in the box. After counting 16 crayons in each of the 4 sections, we are able to say that sixteen 4 times must equal sixty-four, or 16 x 4 = 64.

When another student noticed the 4 neat rows of crayons from left to right across the box, we again confirm the fact that 16 x 4 = 64. Next, someone suggested we count the number of rows of 4 crayons from the front of the box to the back. We counted 16 rows of 4 for a total of 64 crayons once again but this time 4 x 16 = 64. From this we surmise that multiplication works both ways like addition; we discover that multiplication is commutative.

From this box of crayons we are also able to show:

> 8 rows of 8 crayons, or 8 x 8 = 64
> 1 crayon 64 times for 1 x 64 = 64 and 64 x 1 = 64.
> 32 rows of 2, or 32 x 2 = 64 and 2 x 32 =64

We attach sticky notes to the box to illustrate the different multiplication sentences that have a product of 64. On another day, students use their own box of 16 crayons (adapt the lesson to suit the number of crayons available to students or provide extra crayons to small groups of students) to help illustrate different multiplication sentences using the idea of repeated addition. To illustrate the number sentence 4x4, for example, students arrange four groups of four crayons for a total of 16 crayons. Crayons are wonderful companion manipulatives to a multiplication practice sheet and make this math concept fun and concrete.

Our Box of 64 Crayola Crayons

Another Art Lesson: Borrowing Illustration Techniques

Tommy knew that real artists didn't copy, so why did the art teacher, Mrs. Bowers, ask the class to copy her Pilgrim man, Pilgrim woman, and a turkey? Perhaps for the same reason that I send my frustrated artists to look at our collection of favorite books when faced with a particularly difficult illustration. Seeing how an expert tackled a similar problem when drawing (or writing) provides a level of comfort and usually prevents some of the hopeless erasing demonstrated by many young artists. In fact, this whole idea of "borrowing" techniques from the authors of children's literature is what began my literature-based classroom in the first place.

To help students gain confidence in their illustrations, I tell them that sometimes it's okay to be a copy cat. With this in mind, we turn to Tomie dePaola's *The Art Lesson* to see just what kinds of things we could learn to draw from examining this book. I encourage students to turn to favorite books for help with any illustrating dilemma. I explain how these expert authors and illustrators are always ready to lend a hand with art lessons.

Helpful Illustrating Hints from *The Art Lesson*

- the back of a cat
- someone doing cartwheels and head stands
- a grocery store
- a windy day
- a classroom
- kids in "school clothes"
- a teacher
- a boy in bed
- a Pilgrim man and woman
- a turkey

Doing Favorite Things:
Identifying Verbs as Action Words

Tommy's friends had favorite things to do, too. Jack collected all kinds of turtles. Herbie made huge cities in his sandbox. Jeannie, Tommy's best friend, could do cartwheels and stand on her head. But Tommy drew and drew and drew. Everyone has a very favorite thing to do. Students and I compile a list of our favorite things to see the diversity of our interests as well as the *-ing* ending that is common to action words or verbs. Our completed list of "Favorite Things to Do" looks something like the one shown at right.

New action words are added to our list as they arise in books, conversation, and our own actions. We discuss how silent 'e' is dropped from the end of words before *-ing* is added. We add this list to our reference charts for use during writing time.

Doing Favorite Things

- ☀ hiking
- ☀ reading
- ☀ doing cartwheels
- ☀ drawing
- ☀ collecting baseball cards
- ☀ playing football
- ☀ playing soccer
- ☀ writing stories
- ☀ coloring with crayons
- ☀ painting
- ☀ jumping rope
- ☀ riding bikes
- ☀ cooking
- ☀ helping my mom and dad
- ☀ eating pizza
- ☀ playing with my toys
- ☀ watching t.v.
- ☀ playing with friends
- ☀ playing outside

No More Painting on the Walls: Painting Murals of School Activities

"No more painting on the walls" Tomie's father told him when the painters arrived. But what if the walls are covered in butcher paper? To give my students an opportunity to paint on the walls, I hang butcher paper outside our classroom. Next, I have students recall favorite highlights from our school year to date. I label sections of the paper with these memories. A unit kick-off or end-of-unit celebration, field trip, special guest, or activity are some of the ideas I will write at the top of the paper.

Groups of students, armed with paint brushes, paint sections of the mural. If possible, a parent volunteer may supervise one small group of painters at a time while the teacher works with the remaining students on another activity. New paper can be hung and ideas added as the year progresses. The result is a colorful display for the hallway that has students asking for time for "more painting on the walls."

More Books by Tomie dePaola

Big Anthony and the Magic Ring (Harcourt Brace Jovanovich, 1979)

Bonjour Mr. Satie (G.P. Putnam's Sons, 1991)

Charlie Needs a Cloak (Half Moon Books, 1973)

Days of the Blackbird (G.P. Putnam's Sons, 1997)

The Knight and the Dragon (Putnam & Grosset Group, 1980)

Merry Christmas, Strega Nona (Harcourt Brace Jovanovich, 1986)

Michael Bird-Boy (Prentice Hall Books for Young Readers, 1975)

Nana Upstairs & Nana Downstairs (G.P. Putnam's Sons, 1993)

Strega Nona Her Story (G.P. Putnam's Sons, 1996)

Strega Nona's Magic Lessons (Harcourt Brace Jovanovich, 1982)

Strega Nona Meets Her Match (G.P. Putnam's Sons, 1993)

Tom (G.P. Putnam's Sons, 1993)

Watch Out for the Chicken Feet in Your Soup (Prentice-Hall, Inc., 1974)

Name _____ Date _____

As Colorful as a Crayon

Boxes of 64 Crayola Crayons have colorful names like carnation pink, dandelion yellow, macaroni and cheese orange, and robin's egg blue. On the crayons below, write analogies to describe 5 crayons in your crayon box. Color each crayon using the newly named color.

as _____ as a _____

as _____ as a _____

as _____ as a _____

as _____ as a _____

as _____ as a _____

100 Skill-Building Lessons Using 10 Favorite Books   Scholastic Professional

Name _____ Date _____

✫ ✩ ✫ As Happy as a Clam ✩ ✫
and Other Analogies to Describe Feelings

On the lines below, practice writing analogies to describe feelings.
Or, use the recording sheet to record other analogies you discover
in your reading and writing that describe feelings.

as _____ as a _____

as _____ as a _____

as _____ as a _____

as _____ as a _____

as _____ as a _____

as _____ as a _____

Chapter Seven

I Don't Want to Share My Stuff...

LESSONS 61 TO 70

Top Cat
by Lois Ehlert

Mini-Lessons Across the Curriculum

Language Arts

Scrambled Sentences	*Using context clues*
Unscrambling Top Cat	*Practicing with context clues*
I'm Top Cat	*Identifying contractions*
Top Cat Sleeps Over	*A journal-writing activity*
Top Cat Poems	*Writing shape poems*

Math & Science

Growing Catnip	*Nurturing and measuring plants*
Top Cat Math	*Using manipulatives to solve math problems*

Community

Feline Friends	*Building a classroom community*

Art

Collage Art	*Exploring texture and color*
Top Cat Puppets	*Retelling stories through puppet shows*

Scrambled Sentences

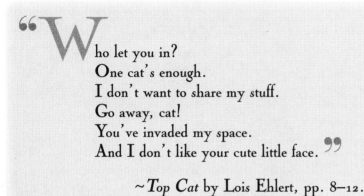
GOAL *Using Context Clues*

> "Who let you in?
> One cat's enough.
> I don't want to share my stuff.
> Go away, cat!
> You've invaded my space.
> And I don't like your cute little face."
>
> ~*Top Cat* by Lois Ehlert, pp. 8–12.

The collage illustrations, the simple rhyming text, and the way Lois Ehlert accurately portrays the independent, moody, cantankerous, playful nature of cats combine to make *Top Cat* a delightful read-aloud. The fact that this book is a wonderful companion to *Feathers for Lunch* makes *Top Cat* a favorite of my young readers.

After reading *Top Cat* for the first time, my students enjoy convincing one another that the main character cat from Lois Ehlert's *Feathers for Lunch* is making another appearance in *Top Cat*. The added texture in the illustrations of *Top Cat* cause some readers to question whether these two cats are one in the same, although both cats are black with white markings on the face, have white-tipped tails and yellow eyes. The bell and heart on the blue collar is exactly the same in both books. One very astute supporter of the same character theory notes that Top Cat allowed the new kitten to venture outside alone when the "door's left open," which proves that Top Cat is the "Feathers for Lunch cat"—he knew it was almost dinnertime and didn't want to risk getting just feathers for lunch again.

After discussing the same cats/different cats theory, we read *Top Cat* many times in many ways (teacher read-aloud with students filling in the missing words, class choral readings, etc.). The short, simple, rhyming text makes numerous rereadings possible and students quickly know *Top Cat* "inside out and upside down."

To accommodate the different ability levels in my class, I scramble the text first by lines then by the words in lines. In the lesson that follows, I combine both techniques. You may wish to scramble the entire poem by lines and save the word by word part for another day. The basic steps to this scrambled word strategy are:

1. Help students become familiar with the poem or text to be manipulated.

2. Scramble text line by line. Put back together. Read words in order.

3. Scramble text word by word. Put back together. Read words in order.

Once the students are familiar with *Top Cat*, we are ready for our "scrambled sentences" mini-lesson, which increases sight word vocabulary, provides exposure to new words as well as rhyming word pairs, and allows students to play with words in the context of a favorite book. I make a transparency of the *Top Cat* text, cut it apart, and place it on the overhead projector (or I might copy the text onto oak tag sentence strips and place in scrambled order on a pocket chart as shown below—see tip on page 101).

For the independent practice, give students a copy of the second half of the text, a plain piece of white paper, envelopes for storing extra pieces, and glue sticks. A copy of the complete text for small groups to share is helpful, as well. With these preparations complete, gather students for a lesson on scrambled sentences that helps them use context clues and rhyming words to figure out "what makes sense" when reading.

Ready for Our Scrambled Sentences Lesson ▷

Mrs. L.:	Would you please help me read the words on the chart from *Top Cat?*
Class:	*Who let you in? One cat's enough.* *And I don't want to share my stuff.* *Boring job! Never see a mouse.* *Nothing much happens in this dull house.*
Ben:	The lines are mixed up.
Madison:	The next two lines are really the first words of *Top Cat.*
Mrs. L.:	How can you tell? The words at the ends of the lines still rhyme.
David:	Because you don't know what Top Cat's boring job is until you hear him say he guards the place in his coat of fur. Those words have to come first.
Mrs. L.:	Let's move the first two lines to the top of the chart...Now read the words again.
Class:	*I'm top cat. Pet me, I'll purr.* *I guard this place in my coat of fur.* *Boring job! Never see a mouse.* *Nothing much happens in this dull house.*

Mrs. L.:	That sounds better. Let's keep reading.
	Go away, cat! You've invaded my space.
	And I don't like your cute little face.
Molly:	That's out of order. First we need the part where Top Cat meets the new cat. The words at the bottom.
Mrs. L.:	Let's read those words together.
Class:	*Who let you in? One cat's enough.*
	I don't want to share my stuff.
Mrs. L.:	Molly, would you please put this part in the correct order…Now let's read the words again…
Class:	*I'm top cat. Pet me, I'll purr.*
	I guard this place in my coat of fur.
	Boring job! Never see a mouse.
	Nothing much happens in this dull house.
	Who let you in? One cat's enough.
	I don't want to share my stuff.
	Go away, cat! You've invaded my space.
	And I don't like your cute little face.
Mary:	That's better.
Mrs. L.:	Now it sounds like Lois Ehlert's version to me, too. Here are the next few lines of the story. Read them with me, please.
Class:	*Well, you're here to stay. I can see that.*
	I'll fight you and bite you behind the ear.
Hannah:	That's not the right order. I'll fight you and bite you behind the ear comes first.
Mrs. L.:	Could you please move this line under the completed part of the chart, Hannah?
Hannah:	Sure. Well, *you're here to stay* isn't the next line.
Tyler:	You can tell because *that* and *ear* don't rhyme.
Mrs. L.:	Good thinking, Tyler. What line does rhyme with the word *ear*?
Tyler:	The one that ends with *here*.

We continue putting the lines in order, using our memories and rhyming clues to help us.

Mrs. L.:	There are a few other things Top Cat wants to teach striped cat. Let me put a few other lines up here for you to help me put in the correct order. Read the next two lines and tell me which line comes next:
Class:	*Drink there. from sink company's when the*
	with table the the on silverware. Dance
Collin:	That doesn't make any sense.
Matthew:	The words are out of order.
Mrs. L.:	You're right! We need to put these words back in order to tell what Top Cat and Striped Cat do next. Do you see any key words in the first line?
Samantha:	*Drink* and *sink*. I wasn't sure what the word c-o-m-p-a-n-y is. Then I remembered they drank from the sink when company was there.

Mrs. L.:	Excellent! Samantha, would you please put these words in order for us? The rest of you think about the order for the next line.
Emma:	I see the words *silverware* and *dance*. The next line is *they dance with the silverware.*
Mrs. L.:	Would you like to put this sentence back together for us?
Emma:	Sure. It should be *Dance on the table with the silverware.*
Mrs. L.:	Great! Let's do one more line together before you give this a try on your own. Look for key words in the next two lines, please.
Class:	*Go some open? air. Door's get fresh left*
Matthew:	*Door* has to be the first word because it's a capital 'D.'
Mrs. L.:	That's a great hint to use, Matthew. Let's move *Door's* to the beginning of the line. Are there other hints?
Samantha:	There's a question mark after the word *open*. It must be the last word in the line.
Eric:	But there's also a period after the word *air*.
Elizabeth:	And a capital 'G' for *Go*. Maybe it's the first word in this line.
Mrs. L.:	This is the line where Top Cat asks a question and answers himself. So there are two thoughts in this one line of text.
David:	I think he asks *Is the door left open?*
Lauren:	There's no *is*. It's just *Door's left open*. Like *Feathers for Lunch*.
Mrs. L.:	I think you're right. Let's move these words around. What's the next line?

We confirm the remaining lines.

Mrs. L.:	Now I think it's time for you to test your memories and give this a try on your own.

Independent Practice

Unscrambling Top Cat: Practicing with Context Clues

Mrs. L.:	I'll give you a paper with the words from the end of *Top Cat* scrambled. Cut the words apart then unscramble them on another sheet of paper. Glue the words onto the paper once you're sure they are in the correct order. Feel free to refer to our charted version of *Top Cat* for help with placing the words so they are just right.

I send students to their seats with copies of the text and blank sheets of white paper. I place the *Top Cat* Chart in a place where all can see (or make a transparency to place on the overhead), and then I walk around the room giving reminders to check before gluing words on paper and assisting as needed. The students rearrange two sections of words as demonstrated in the mini-lesson then work to unscramble more words so that:

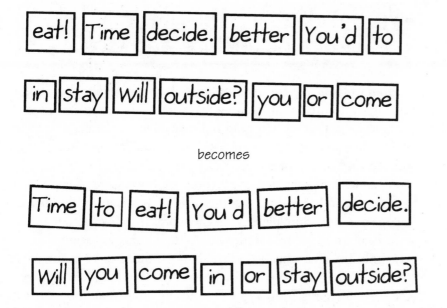

becomes

As students arrive the following morning, the final scrambled part of *Top Cat* is made available to cut and paste in the correct order:

| Let's | milk | Welcome | drink | our | back! | furs | in. |

| Just | no | No | no | scratches, | hisses, | bites. | purrs. |

Unscrambling Top Cat ▷

8 More Book-Based Lessons

Collage Art: Exploring Texture and Color

The illustrations of *Top Cat* are an inspiration to young artists who enjoy experimenting with different art techniques. Prior to the art lesson, I cut main shapes of the cat's body and head but save a few minor parts (such as the tail, eyes, and ears) to demonstrate for students. A white shape for the face and the tip of the tail, yellow eyes, thin gray whiskers, a pink nose, and a triangular collar will complete my collage of Top Cat.

Our lesson begins as I tack the large body shape and head/neck to a large piece of white paper with the words *Top Cat* written at the top. I call on individual students to glue the shapes together to assemble Top Cat. I send students back to their seats bearing paper from our scrap box to make their own toy mouse, like the one on the cover dangling from Top Cat's mouth. This small mouse makes a wonderful first attempt at collage for young artists.

Our art center for the next week allows students to hone their collage cutting and pasting technique, using the pages of *Top Cat* for inspiration as they try a hand at making Striped Cat and Top Cat in the different poses found on the pages of this delightful book.

◀ *Our Class Top Cat*

Top Cat Art Center Creations

Top Cat Puppets: Retelling Stories Through Puppet Shows

Attach craft sticks to the animals from the Collage Art activity described on page 104 and students have puppets for a "Top Cat Meets Striped Cat" puppet show. Students can work at the art center to make additional collage puppets for Top Cat and Striped Cat and other props such as birds, silverware, mice, balls, etc. Small groups of students can rehearse short plays that retell the original story or present new adventures of these two feline friends. When rehearsals are complete, the plays can be performed for the rest of the class. The stage can be as simple as puppets raised up from behind desks or a table top with puppeteers hiding underneath. This activity makes a great rainy day art project for indoor recess, and students love creating the puppets and performing the stories.

Top Cat Puppets

I'm Top Cat: Identifying Contractions

The text of *Top Cat* provides opportunities on nearly every page for discussing the use of contractions. I give one copy to each student and make an overhead transparency of the text for this word study lesson. As individual students are called to the overhead to circle words that have an apostrophe, the rest of the class copies the word on individual recording sheets. Above each contraction we write the two words that make up the contraction (above the word *I'm* we write the two words *I am*).

We discuss how contractions shorten two words into one word and sound more conversational, flow more easily, and sound more rhythmic when read aloud. Without contractions, "I'm Top Cat. Pet me, I'll purr" would be "I am Top Cat. Pet me and I will purr." When we are finished, the words we have lengthened within the context of the story are:

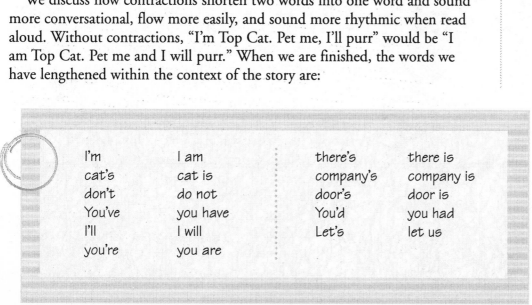

I'm	I am	there's	there is
cat's	cat is	company's	company is
don't	do not	door's	door is
You've	you have	You'd	you had
I'll	I will	Let's	let us
you're	you are		

Growing Catnip:
Nurturing and Measuring Plants

Give students an opportunity to grow some new treats for "top cats" they know with an ongoing science lesson in growing and measuring plants. Have each student fill a Styrofoam cup with soil, drop in a few catnip (or grass) seeds, and mist the newly planted seeds with water. After students decorate the cup as desired with markers—perhaps with illustrations of Top Cat—place the plants in an out-of-the-way place near a sunny window, if possible. Water as needed until Top Cat's favorite snacks have grown.

For a different twist on this lesson, have small groups plant a few seeds in cups. Label one cup as "A" and place it in a bright sunny window and water appropriately. Label another cup as "B" and place it in a dark corner of the room and water appropriately. Label a third cup as "C" and place it in a closet with water. Cup "D" could be placed in the sunny window without giving water. Have your young scientists hypothesize and create other possible test plant situations then make predictions regarding the likelihood of good growth, or rank them in order from least to most likely to grow. Copies of the "Growing Catnip for Top Cat" reproducible (page 109) can be used for recording the growth of these plants.

Top Cat and a friend share his journal with the class.

Top Cat Sleeps Over:
A Journal-Writing Activity

Even students who are allergic to cats will be allowed to take part in this activity, which allows them to take Top Cat home for the night. At the end of each day, I announce whose turn it is to take Top Cat, our stuffed black cat mascot, home. This little black cat travels with his backpack filled with all the things needed for a sleep over: his blanket, toothbrush, and special toy mouse.

Of course, Top Cat never leaves school without his journal, special pencil, and box of crayons so that he can do his homework. Each night Top Cat must write about the day's adventure with the help of his student host or hostess. One morning Top Cat returned to school sporting a bandage and the journal entry detailed his dreadful encounter with the family's new puppy.

As his sleep-over buddy reads his journal entry to the rest of the class, Top Cat takes a cat nap on top of our box of favorite books until the end of the day when he will go home with another member of the class.

Feline Friends:
Building a Classroom Community

The following activities are designed to acquaint your students with those top cats who grace the lives of classmates with their furs, purrs, and occasional scratches and hisses:

1. Invite a special guest to share a Top Cat or two. Contact a local pet shop, veterinarian office, or humane society to arrange for a guest speaker to visit with a few feline friends and have a discussion of cat care. Prior to the visit, have students compile a list of questions to ask the speaker at the end of the presentation.

Mrs. L's "Top Cat."

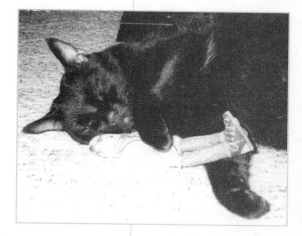

2. Prepare a bulletin board of class Feline Friends where students display pictures brought from home of their cats. Enlist the help of students without pet cats to make a border for the bulletin board—a pattern of fish-shaped cat treats, mouse toys, and balls of yarn, for example. Students may fill out the form on page 110 to describe their pet and share this information with the class prior to placing on the bulletin board.

3. Have a Cat Week where parents or caregivers may bring the family feline in for a short visit to meet the class. These visits are all arranged ahead of time and allow students to share their special family cat.

Top Cat Math:
Using Manipulatives
to Solve Math Problems

Make a collection of cat-related math manipulatives by filling small containers with fish-shaped crackers, jingle bells, and fish-shaped candies ("Swedish Fish") to make solving the Top Cat Math problems found on page 111 more fun.

Although the problems require that students solve addition and subtraction facts to 20, they can easily be adapted to other skill levels and math concepts. Be sure to include enough counters for students to help Top Cat do the math. If readability is a problem, have students manipulate the counters as you read the problems aloud.

Doing Top Cat Math ▶

Top Cat Poems: Writing Shape Poems

Hissing, purring, scratching, meowing. Cat words provide young students with an opportunity to play with language and make cat-shaped "poems."

Begin by brainstorming a list of describing words for cats. Perusing the pages of *Top Cat* could elicit a list of words such as the ones shown below.

Next, have students outline a very basic shape of a cat on a piece of construction or writing paper with a pencil. Students then select their favorite cat words to write around the outline. For added texture and fun, have students add pipe-cleaner or yarn whiskers, collage cut-out eyes, or a jingle-bell collar before displaying these Top Cat Poems in the hallway or on a bulletin board.

Eric's Top Cat Poem

hissing	chomping	adorable
padded-feet	furry	biting
purring	milk-lapping	clawing
leaping	soft	sandpapered-tongue
scratching	dancing	licking
bouncing	playful	striped
meowing	stalking	scritching
shedding	tail-swishing	
arched-back	pawing	

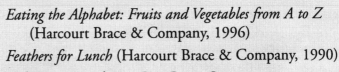

More Books by Lois Ehlert

Eating the Alphabet: Fruits and Vegetables from A to Z
(Harcourt Brace & Company, 1996)

Feathers for Lunch (Harcourt Brace & Company, 1990)

Fish Eyes: A Book You Can Count On
(Harcourt Brace & Company, 1990)

Growing Vegetable Soup (Harcourt Brace Jovanovich, 1987)

Nuts to You (Harcourt Brace Jovanovich, 1993)

Planting a Rainbow (Harcourt Brace & Company, 1988)

Snowballs (Harcourt Brace & Company, 1995)

Name _____ Date _____

Growing Catnip for Top Cat

A chart for recording the growth of a plant you grow for your favorite Top Cat.

On _____ , I planted my catnip plant.
Here is what I did:

1. _____

2. _____

3. _____

Here is a picture
of my plant.

Date: _____

New information about my plant:

_____

_____

My plant measures _____ cm.

Here is a picture
of my plant:

Date: _____

New information about my plant:

_____

_____

My plant measures _____ cm.

Here is a picture
of my plant:

Date: _____

New information about my plant:

_____

_____

My plant measures _____ cm.

Here is a picture
of my plant:

Date: _____

New information about my plant:

_____

_____

My plant measures _____ cm.

Here is a picture
of my plant:

Name _____ Date _____

_____'s Top Cat

(attach a photo
of your Top Cat here)

My cat's full name is _____.

We adopted my cat on _____.

My cat's favorite place to nap is _____.

My cat's favorite thing to play with is _____.

My cat's favorite food is _____.

My cat's bad habit is _____.

My cat purrs when _____.

My cat hisses when _____.

The funniest thing my cat ever did was _____

_____.

My cat is extra-special because _____

_____.

100 Skill-Building Lessons Using 10 Favorite Books   Scholastic Professional Books

Scholastic Professional Books · 100 Skill-Building Lessons Using 10 Favorite Books

Name _____ Date _____

Top Cat Math

Directions: Use addition or subtraction to solve the problems below.

1. While Top Cat was guarding the house in his coat of fur, he chased away 12 birds from the window. He batted at 3 flies and hissed at 1 Striped Cat. How many animals did Top Cat encounter while guarding his house?

2. Top Cat doesn't want to share his stuff, so he is taking an inventory of his toys. He found 6 little balls under the bed. He found 4 play mice under the sofa. He found 8 feather toys on top of the table. How many toys does Top Cat have all together?

3. If Striped Cat carried away 3 of Top Cat's toys, how many toys does Top Cat have left?

4. Even though there's more to do than eat and sleep, Top Cat and Striped Cat napped for 5 hours. Then they chased the birds. They napped for 3 more hours. Then they chased some more birds. Then they napped for 2 more hours. How many hours did Top Cat and Striped Cat nap?

5. Top Cat wanted to eat plants till the leaves were bare. Top Cat found a plant with 15 leaves. He ate 11 of the leaves. How many leaves are left on the tree?

6. Top Cat and Striped Cat like to drink from the sink when company's there. Top Cat drank 12 drops from the leaky facet. Striped Cat drank 8 drops of water. How many drops of water did they drink all together?

7. When Top Cat and Striped Cat were drinking from the sink, they each broke 6 dishes. How many dishes did they break all together?

8. Striped Cat went out to get some fresh air. He saw 20 birds sitting in the tree. 9 of the birds flew away. How many birds were left in the tree?

Chapter Eight

Lucky to Have a Special Friend

LESSONS 71 TO 80

Best Friends
by Steven Kellogg

Mini-Lessons Across the Curriculum

Language Arts

Problems at Pine Cone Peak	*Solving problems in written stories*
Staying Best Friends	*Practicing solving problems*
Meet Golden Silverwind	*Writing puppy birth announcements*
Wished, Pretended, Promised	*Studying words with -ed endings*

Math & Science

A Dog's Day	*Telling time in 15-minute intervals*
Puppy Problems	*Solving story problems*

Community

A Best Friends Party	*Building community through positive reinforcement*
My Magic Hat	*Sharing wishes and dreams*
The Ups and Downs of Friendship	*Using "I Feel" statements to resolve conflicts*

Art

Face-to-Face Friends	*Drawing portraits of friends*

Problems at Pine Cone Peak

GOAL *Solving Problems in Written Stories*

> "It wasn't fair. She wasn't lonely like me. She wasn't missing me at all. Louise Jenkins was a traitor! She was my worst friend. I wished that a volcanic eruption would blast Pine Cone Peak into Pebbles..."
>
> ~*Best Friends* by Steven Kellogg, pp. 12–13.

Best Friends by Steven Kellogg is a perfect book to read when trying to help young children deal with two problems that often plague them in first, second, and third grade. One of the problems is dealing with the love-hate emotions that often go hand-in-hand with "best" friendships. I read *Best Friends* for read-aloud the day Hannah realized her best friend, Madison, was having too much fun with Stephanie at recess. Rather than asking if she could join them, Hannah told Madison and Stephanie she hoped they fell off their swings. Talking about Kathy's feelings toward Louise Jenkins in *Best Friends* gave us a safe outlet for discussing the delicate issue of jealousy in friendship and how best to handle such emotions.

The other issue *Best Friends* helps us deal with is of a more academic nature—solving problems in written stories before ending them. One of my favorite illustrations of this problem is illustrated in this "complete" writers' workshop story shared several years ago:*

> One day I was a little scared. When I was in the woods.
> I was chopping wood. I saw a foot. It was a dinosaur's!!!!!!!

The author of this story felt the problem of the story was discovering who the foot belonged to and so this story was, in his eyes, complete. I explained to this young writer that once the audience discovers the foot belongs to a dinosaur, then there is a whole new problem to be solved. "What happened

---

*From *Literature-Based Mini-Lessons to Teach Writing*, Scholastic Professional Books, 1998.

The story *Best Friends* is a story told in the first person by a little girl whose best friend is Louise Jenkins. Before reading the story aloud, I challenge my students to listen carefully to find out the name of Louise's best friend— the friend telling the story. Students are usually quick to pick up on the other best friend's first name when she receives a postcard from Louise on page 11 that begins "Dear Kathy."

Using the names "Kathy" and "Louise" in the mini-lesson that follows makes the discussion easier. So offer the best-friends-name-challenge to your students and clarify the characters' names prior to the mini-lesson. Otherwise, you will be forced to refer to "Kathy" as "the best friend telling the story" or "Louise's best friend," throughout the course of the mini-lesson.

next?" I asked. After adding an entire row of exclamation marks he wrote the words:

> I ran. I jumped into bed. I was safe.

A simple solution, perhaps, but the problem of the story was solved. When I see evidence that my students could benefit from a lesson on story endings, I reach for *Best Friends* and begin a writers' workshop mini-lesson that gives my students some hints about solving problems with friends and in their story writing. Our writers' workshop mini-lesson usually goes something like this:

Mrs. L.: When I read the book *Best Friends* yesterday for read-aloud, I noticed that Steven Kellogg had to solve a lot of problems when he wrote this story.

Lauren: Yes. The little girl in the story didn't get a puppy when Sarah had puppies.

Mrs. L.: You're right. And that's just one of the problems. Today we're going to take a closer look at *Best Friends* to discover the different problems these friends face throughout the story. I'm hoping you will get some ideas about how to solve the problems in the stories that you write. On the board I'll write the problems and the solutions you discover in *Best Friends*. Let's take a look at the first problem. I'll show you the pages to refresh your memories.

Stephanie: That's the page where Louise's aunt and uncle come to get her.

Mrs. L.: Tell me more.

Stephanie: They are taking her away for the summer and she doesn't want to go and Kathy doesn't want her to go.

Mrs. L.: Does this problem get solved?

Sam: Yes, she ends up having a good time.

Lauren: And she comes home again.

Mrs. L.: Louise's best friend, Kathy, thinks of a few other ways to solve this problem of getting Louise home so that she wouldn't have to miss her anymore. Listen as I read this page:

> If only Louise would be able to escape. I even wished she'd get a contagious disease so they'd have to let her come home. I wouldn't be afraid of catching it. I'd nurse her back to health with chocolate milk. I missed her so much! I wished that Golden Silverwind and I could rescue her!

Anna: Those things didn't happen. She just wished they would happen.

Mrs. L.: Right. I like the creative thinking that Steven Kellogg did to help us understand how very much Kathy wanted Louise to come home.

Ben: So much that she'd get around her if she had a contagious disease!

Mrs. L.: Exactly! This must have been a very big problem to Kathy.

Alex: The next problem happens when she gets the postcard and finds out Louise is really having a really fun time.

Mrs. L.: The best summer of her life are the words used to describe how much fun she is having.

Alex: And Louise was making lots of new friends.

Mrs. L.: Louise Jenkins is a traitor! She was my worst friend. I wished that a volcanic eruption would blast Pine Cone Peak into pebbles.

Jack: That would be one way to solve the problem!

Mrs. L.: Maybe there's a better solution. Like having someone new move in across the street.

Matthew: Or, fifty kids her age all with horses.

Mrs. L.: But the problem is that the new person in the house across the street—

David: Is just one old man.

Stephanie: But that problem gets better because he has a dog that's going to have puppies.

Mrs. L.: Tell me why this is a good solution.

Stephanie: Because Kathy's mom says she can have one of the puppies, too.

Jack: That causes a new problem.

Mrs. L.: Tell me about it.

Jack: Mrs. Jenkins orders a puppy for Louise.

We continue discussing the problems presented in the book.

Mrs. L.: Let's take a look at our chart of problems and solutions for Best Friends.

Problems and Solutions for Best Friends

Problem	Solution
1. Louise goes to Pine Cone Peak. Kathy misses her.	☼ Help Louise escape? ☼ Louise gets contagious disease and has to come home? ☼ Golden Silverwind and Kathy rescue Louise?
2. Louise has the best summer of her life. Kathy still misses her.	☼ Volcanic eruption could blast Pine Cone Peak into pebbles? ☼ House across the street is sold to someone new. ☼ Will it be 50 new best friends with real horses?
3. Someone new is just one old man named Mr. Jode.	☼ Mr. Jode has a dog named Sarah who is about to have puppies. Kathy's mom says she may have one.
4. Sarah has only one puppy. It's not a spotted puppy. Louise gets the puppy.	☼ Louise suggests they share the puppy. Name him Golden Silverwind. Mr. Jode builds a dog house between their houses. Mr. Jode and Sarah help with puppy training.
5. Kathy feels guilty for being mad at Louise.	☼ She realizes she is lucky to have a special friend.
6. Louise will go away to Pine Cone Peak next summer.	☼ She will have Golden Silverwind all to herself.

Independent Practice

Staying Best Friends: Practicing Solving Problems

Mrs. L.: When Steven Kellogg was writing the story *Best Friends*, he had to be creative when coming up with solutions to the problems he wrote about.

Lauren: Like when Sarah only had one puppy but two kids each wanted a dog.

Mrs. L.: Exactly. Writers need to create interesting problems for their characters to solve in creative ways so that readers believe the characters' actions and will continue reading the story. For example, I like how Steven Kellogg added Kathy's silly solutions for some of her problems—

Eric: Like when she wanted Louise to get a contagious disease so that she would have to come home.

Matthew: Or blasting Pine Cone Peak to pebbles.

Mrs. L.: Even though these weren't real solutions, they sounded like something Kathy might really think so they help us understand her better.

David: Or helped us think of other crazy ideas in our own minds.

Mrs. L.: Right! That's what I want you to do right now. I've created some story problems that a writer could create. Your job as the writer is to come up with two possible solutions for each problem.

Tyler: Do we write the entire story now?

Mrs. L.: No, just a sentence or two that tells the main idea. You can work with a partner to come up with the possible endings. Let's do one together. Read the first problem with me:

Class: *Golden Silverwind ate Louise's homework paper while it was Kathy's turn to puppy-sit.*

Elizabeth: I think Kathy should help Louise with the homework.

Molly: Kathy needs to be a better puppy-sitter!

Mrs. L.: Tell me how she could do that.

Molly: Well, maybe Golden Silverwind was hungry because she forgot to give him a snack so he decided to eat the homework paper.

Emma: My mom would tell me I should keep my paper in a safer place with a puppy around.

Mrs. L.: I could imagine my dog, Jordan, eating my papers if I left them in an unsafe place. So, our solutions are...

Hannah: Have the girls work together on the homework then talk to their teacher about what happened.

Madison: Tell Kathy to give Golden Silverwind a snack because he must be hungry.

Samantha: Have Louise keep her homework in a better place.

Problem	Possible Solutions
Golden Silverwind ate Louise's homework paper while it was Kathy's turn to puppy-sit.	**1.** Girls work together to redo homework. **2.** Kathy gives Golden Silverwind a snack. **3.** Louise puts homework in her backpack and zips it up.

Mrs. L.: Good solutions. Now, with a partner, choose one of the following problems to solve in at least two different ways. Take a minute to jot down your solutions on the paper I give you. We'll take a few minutes to share your ideas before you begin working on the problems you've created in your own writers' workshop stories.

Problems

- Golden Silverwind chased Mrs. Nevin's cat up a tree again.
- Mr. Jode is going to Florida to visit his sister. His sister lives in an apartment that does not allow pets. What will he do with Sarah?
- Golden Silverwind gets sprayed by a skunk while on his daily walk with his two girls.
- Next summer, when Louise goes to Pine Cone Peak, Kathy's mother's Aunt Fanny pays a visit. They soon discover she is allergic to dogs. She is staying for two whole weeks.

Highlights from the students' creative solutions are shown on the following page. Their work with the story *Best Friends* helped them realize there is more than one way to solve a problem. When faced with their own problems in writing, they began to explore more creative solutions and possibilities before writing the words The End.

Problem	Solution
Golden Silverwind chased Mrs. Nevin's cat up a tree again.	☼ Put sticky tape around the tree so the cat can't climb the tree (since Golden Silverwind only wants to play. The cat is not in any danger). ☼ Give Golden Silverwind more exercise. He must really want to run and play. ☼ Take Golden Silverwind to puppy school so he can meet some dog-friends. He needs a friend of his own.
Mr. Jode is going to Florida to visit his sister. His sister lives in an apartment that does not allow pets. What will he do with Sarah? He will miss her so much.	☼ Louise and Kathy will take great care of Golden Silverwind and are happy because each girl gets a dog each day. They take lots of pictures of the two dog friends and send them to Mr. Jode in Florida. ☼ Mr. Jode calls Kathy and Louise to hear Sarah bark and for an update on how she is doing. He sends special dog treats in the mail for her to let her know he misses her.
Golden Silverwind gets sprayed by a skunk while on his walk with his two girls.	☼ Louise and Kathy run to the store for tomato juice—lots of it. They give Golden Silverwind 2 baths: the first one in tomato juice, the second one in nice smelling shampoo. ☼ The girls give Golden Silverwind a bath in perfume and are careful not to let him off his leash while walking him again!
Next summer, when Louise goes to Pine Cone Peak, Kathy's mother's Aunt Fanny pays a visit. They soon discover she is allergic to dogs. She is staying for two whole weeks.	☼ Ask Aunt Fanny to stay in a motel. It's Kathy's time to have Golden Silverwind all to herself. Aunt Fanny will understand. ☼ Golden Silverwind and Kathy will live together in a tent in the backyard while Aunt Fanny visits. In case of bad weather, they'll move in with Mr. Jode.

8 More Book-Based Lessons

Meet Golden Silverwind: Writing Puppy Birth Announcements

The arrival of a new puppy in the family is cause for celebration! Have your students announce the arrival of Golden Silverwind or their own dog by writing a puppy birth announcement. If possible, begin by sharing a birth announcement you have received (or sent) to give students an opportunity to see a "real" announcement and how it is designed.

Next, have students write a birth announcement from copies you have made of page 126., Students then invent the new puppy's birthday and weight, etc. by filling in the blanks on the announcement. A space for a "snapshot" drawing of the new addition is included, as well. The front of the card can be decorated with a colorful border, ribbons, or small drawing.

You may wish to display the puppy birth announcements to share the joy of Golden Silverwind's arrival with other members of the school community.

A Puppy Birth Announcement
▼

A Dog's Day: Telling Time in 15-Minute Intervals

Have students move the hands on individual student clocks to show how fifteen minutes of time passes. Begin with a time on the hour such as 7:00 and say, for example, "At 7:00, Golden Silverwind has his breakfast. At 7:15, he is ready for his morning walk. At 7:30, he likes to play catch with Louise and Cathy. At 7:45, he watches Kathy and Louise get on the bus and ride off to school. At 8:00, he is ready for his morning nap." Students move the hands on their clocks to match the times announced in your story of Golden Silverwind's day.

As a follow-up activity, students may use copies of the blank clocks found on page 127 to record times for a rebus clock story of their own. Students draw the hands on the blank clocks to show various times in Golden Silverwind's routine, cut and glue onto separate sheets of paper, then label with a sentence as shown at right. Be sure to remind students to make the length of the hour and minute hands easy to distinguish. Have students staple individual pages together to make a booklet of clock pages for Golden Silverwind's Day.

Community

My Magic Hat: Sharing Wishes and Dreams

When Kathy arrived at Mr. Jode's house in her magic hat, Mr. Jode said he wished Kathy would use her magic powers to help him find good homes for all of Sarah's puppies. Spread a little magic in your classroom with this activity for making magic hats.

Make a sample hat by using a sheet of construction paper rounded, trimmed, and stapled into a cone-shape (see photo below). Use a hole punch to make holes on either side of the hat and attach yarn or string to be tied under the chin. Have a parent volunteer assist you in fitting students for similar hats and attach string prior to the decorating session. Be sure to include names on hats for ease in distributing later. Provide glitter, glue, and a scrap box of paper and materials for use in decorating the hats. Have a copy of the book *Best Friends* available so students can see a picture of Kathy and Louise's magic hats.

Next, invite students to join you in a circle wearing their magic hats. Have them take turns sharing what magic their hat will help them do. Making puppies or kittens appear on doorsteps, conjuring up new bikes, and creating world peace are just a few of the feats my young magicians would like to perform.

I keep my magic hat nearby and whenever I need to make a wish for quiet students, an organized classroom, or clean desks, I just put on my hat, state my wish, and watch my students perform a little magic of their own!

NOTE: In the story *Best Friends*, Louise and Kathy's "magical witch hats gave (them) the power to make (their) neighborhood anything they wanted it to be." I am careful to omit the word "witch" from the lesson when talking to my students in order to be sensitive to certain beliefs. I do, however, feel it is important for young children to have the opportunity to pretend and feel the "magic" of stretching their imaginations by venturing into the land of make-believe.

Making Magic Hats ▶

A Best Friends Party: Building Community Through Positive Reinforcement

Mr. Jode and Sarah will be helping Louise and Kathy with Golden Silverwind's training. "Train" your students to work cooperatively and they can earn "chips" toward a popcorn-movie party featuring *Best Friends* on Reading Rainbow.*

Simply label a clear container with the words "Best Friends Party" then slide a large colorful rubber band onto the jar approximately one-third of the way up from the bottom of the jar (a clear container such as a Mason jar works best for it allows students to watch the chips accumulate). Explain to the class that when groups of students or the entire class works well together (see suggestions below), you will add a "chip" to the jar (bingo chips, pennies, or other similar items found in your classroom work well for this). When the chips reach the rubber band marker on the jar, "The Best Friends Party" is scheduled for the next convenient day.

I have been known to carry chips around in my pocket, holding one up as needed as a quiet reminder for students to check their behavior or attention. Likewise, one quiet clink of a chip in the jar when it is least expected works wonders to encourage positive behavior in the classroom— "You are all being so considerate of each others' writing time that I think I'll add a chip to the jar."

Once the first goal is reached, slide the rubber band up the jar and have students work for another agreed upon fun day—such as an ice cream party, pizza party, or book buddy time. The goal and what must be accomplished to reach the goal is adaptable to the needs and resources of your classroom.

If you fear your class will have a difficult time reaching a goal due to a few behavior problems in the classroom, make the first goal easily reached. This provides encouragement in meeting the next goal and allows you to say "You did this once, I know you can do it again." Even with the most challenging behavior situations, my classes have always earned their popcorn parties—although one year it took us until November to have the first one!

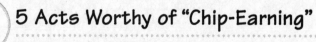

5 Acts Worthy of "Chip-Earning"

1. Working out problems in a reasonable way.

2. Responding to a teacher direction on the first request.

3. Using manners.

4. Walking quietly in the hallways.

5. Cooperating to accomplish a goal.

*Check with your school librarian about securing a copy of or taping this episode of Reading Rainbow for your class.

Two Face-to-Face Friends

Face-to-Face Friends: Drawing Portraits of Friends

Have pairs of students push their desks together or sit across from each other at tables just like Louise and Kathy on page 5 of *Best Friends*. Invite students to draw a picture of this friend while sitting face-to-face. Provide white construction paper "canvases" (page 128) and have students outline their friend from head to shoulders. The challenge for beginning artists is often to "fill up" most of the white space without drawing the model's entire body so it's wise to encourage students to use pencils for this part of the portrait.

When the outline of the friend is complete, have students use watercolor to complete the portrait. Encourage details among artists by having them check eye color, add stripes or decorations to clothing, and add features such as hair clips or glasses. These face-to-face friends make wonderful decorations for the classroom and a keepsake when returned to the model to take home.

Wished, Pretended, Promised: Studying Words with -<u>ed</u> Endings

Use *Best Friends* for a word study mini-lesson in which students find the 28 words with -ed endings that Steven Kellogg used to tell this story. As you reread the book emphasizing -ed words, ask students to give a signal each time they hear one of these words. The signal can be something as simple as saying "stop" to interrupt the reading, holding up a hand or a paper "stop" sign, or snapping a finger.

As students identify the words with -ed, write the words on a chart to discuss after the reading. You may wish to have students copy the words onto a slip of paper or onto individual chalkboards, circling the -ed endings. When you have finished, discuss how the ending -ed changes the tense of the root word. Since Steven Kellogg has Kathy telling a story of something that has already happened to her, she *missed, pretended,* and *wished.* On another day, talk about root words that had to be changed prior to adding -ed: *spot* and *plan* both need an extra letter, and *try* and *worry* need *y* changed to *i* before adding -ed.

This word study lesson helps build students' awareness of the many different words they will encounter in their reading and writing. As more -ed words are discovered in other books and writing, add these to the list and watch your words that tell of things that already happened grow.

allowed	excited	haunted	handed
spotted	shared	seemed	missed IIII
loved	started	scared	tried
promised	pretended II	called	prayed
pushed	planned	turned	worried
showed	wanted III	arrived	asked III
played	interested	wished III	talked

Puppy Problems: Solving Story Problems

Give your students a handful of manipulatives or a piece of scrap paper and have them work on the following problem-solving activities based on the theme of puppies. The problems make great morning work or "mind-stretchers" when written on the board for students to solve as they arrive in the morning. Adapt the following problems to suit your students' needs and levels of understanding. "Puppy School" and "New Toy" problems include graphs to give students a visual to help them in computing the possible solutions. See pages 129 and 130 to make copies for your class.

One Student's Practice Schedule ▶

Puppy Problems: Puppy School

Kathy and Louise are taking Golden Silverwind to puppy school. He is learning how to sit, stay, come when called, and wait. The teacher asks that the girls fill out a weekly practice schedule to ensure that Golden Silverwind gets into a good practice routine. Sometimes the girls forget to fill out the chart. Please help the girls figure out how many minutes they should have worked on the missing days in order to have trained Golden Silverwind a total of 60 minutes each week. The totals must add up to 60 minutes each week.

	Week 1	Week 2	Week 3	Week 4	Week 5
Monday	5	15	10	10	10
Tuesday	15	7	11	10	10
Wednesday	10	10	10	15	0
Thursday	10	10	14	5	10
Friday	10	13	5	15	15
Saturday	6	5	5	20	24
Sunday	4	0	5	5	1
Total minutes	60	60	60	60	60

Use the space below for adding numbers from the above chart.

Puppy Mealtime!

Louise and Kathy are to feed Golden Silverwind three times a day until he is a year old. He needs to get four cups of dog food each day. If there are 50 cups of food in the bag of dog food, how many days will the bag of dog food last?

Walking the Dog

Louise and Kathy are sure to give Golden Silverwind a walk everyday. On school days, they walk him one mile. On Saturday and Sunday, they take him on a 2 mile walk in the morning and a 1 mile walk in the afternoon. How many miles do Golden Silverwind and his girls walk each week?

Puppy School

Kathy and Louise are taking Golden Silverwind to puppy school. He is learning how to sit, stay, come when called, and wait. The teacher asks that the girls fill out a weekly practice schedule to ensure that Golden Siverwind gets into a good practice routine. Sometimes the girls forget to fill out the chart. Please help the girls figure out how many minutes they should have worked on the missing days in order to have worked with their dog a total of 60 minutes each week. The totals must add up to 60 minutes each week (see page 129).

New Toys

Kathy and Louise have saved $8.00 to buy Golden Silverwind some puppy toys and one box of treats from the Pet Store. Look at the toys on page 130 and the price of each. Help the girls decide what they could buy for him and still have $1.50 left to buy him a box of dog treats as rewards for his training. Their mothers have told them to think about saving some change to put toward his next box of dog treats. Think of at least 4 possible ways for the girls to spend their money (see page 130).

The Ups and Downs of Friendship: Using "I Feel" Statements to Resolve Conflicts

Even best friends like Kathy and Louise have times when they don't get along. The situations below involving Kathy and Louise's characters can give your students practice role-playing how to use "I feel" statements when faced with conflicts with their friends.

Ask for volunteers to play the parts of Kathy and Louise and share how they would feel if faced with the given problems. Add two other "best friends" named Kenny and Lewis to get a few boys participating. While one character shares how he or she feels, the other character must listen carefully and then repeat the friend's feelings. Use the example using conflict #1 below to show students how to express feelings using "I feel" statements. The underlined words can be replaced with any words appropriate in a situation.

Rehearsing how to listen to others and to express their own feelings is a worthwhile activity for young children. Getting them to stop and ask "how can we solve this problem" is an important step and a question for the whole class to repeat along with the characters.

Conflict #1

Kathy got a new bike for her birthday. Louise understands that this new present is extra special because it is brand new and it is a gift from her Grandma Cotski. Kathy has not offered a turn to Louise, so Louise decides to borrow the bike when Kathy is eating dinner. After dinner, Kathy finds Louise riding her new bike. Her first instinct is to push Louise off the bike. Instead she takes a deep breath and tells her how she feels.

Student 1 (Kathy):   I feel <u>angry</u> when you <u>take my bike without asking</u>.

Student 2 (Louise):   I hear you saying you feel <u>angry</u> that I <u>took your bike without asking</u>.
But I feel <u>disappointed</u> that you <u>haven't let me ride your new bike</u>.

Kathy and Louise: How can we solve this problem?

After allowing students playing the parts of Kathy and Louise to act out how they would solve the problem, pose the conflict to the entire class and open up a discussion of other possible resolutions to the given conflict.

Possible Resolutions

* Kathy promises to give Louise a turn but asks that she not take her bike again without asking first.

* Louise tells Kathy to play with her favorite doll while she rides Kathy's new bike.

Getting students to use their words to describe the feelings created by another's actions is the first step to resolving conflicts before they escalate to larger conflicts and/or physical problems.

More Conflicts Among Friends

☼ Louise invites a new friend over to play. When Kathy goes to Louise's house, Louise and the new friend do not include Kathy in their game of hopscotch. Kathy runs home crying.

☼ Kathy claims it is her turn to take Golden Silverwind for a walk. Louise says it is her turn. The two girls begin shouting at each other and Golden Silverwind hides under the bed and refuses to come out.

☼ Louise makes fun of Kathy's picture in art class so Kathy tells Louise that her new sweater is ugly.

☼ Sarah is expecting a new litter of puppies. Both Louise and Kathy want a new puppy and to keep Golden Silverwind. Their moms agree that two dogs in the house at the same time is too much but tell the girls if they can work it out between them, they are allowed to have one puppy as a friend to Golden Silverwind. How can Louise and Kathy solve this problem?

More Books by Steven Kellogg

Chicken Little (Morrow Junior Books, 1985)

I Was Born About 10,000 Years Ago (Morrow Junior Books, 1996)

Much Bigger Than Martin (Dial Books for Young Readers, 1976)

The Mystery of the Missing Red Mitten (The Dial Press, 1974)

Pinkerton, Behave! (The Dial Press, 1979)

Prehistoric Pinkerton (Dial Books for Young Readers, 1987)

Ralph's Secret Weapon (Dial Books for Young Readers, 1983)

Tallyho, Pinkerton (The Dial Press, 1979)

The Three Little Pigs (Morrow Junior Books, 1997)

Announcing the Arrival of our Puppy

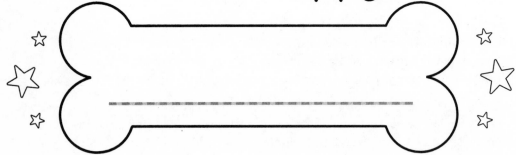

Born on _____

_____ pounds

On the night we brought our puppy home,

_____

_____

Here is a picture of our newest family member:

100 Skill-Building Lessons Using 10 Favorite Books   Scholastic Professional Books

A Day in the Life of Golden Silverwind

Draw the hands on the clocks below to show 5 parts of Golden Silverwind's daily routine. Practice telling time by describing events that happen on the hour and at a quarter past, half-past, and quarter till the hour in your story.

Cut and glue the clocks onto paper and write a sentence telling what Golden Silverwind does each day at the times you have depicted.

Include a picture of Golden Silverwind at each of these times doing the activity described.

At 5:15, Golden Silverwind eats his dinner.

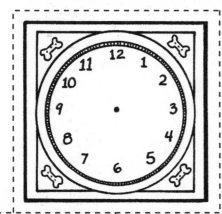 

  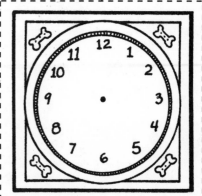

Face-to-Face Friends

On the canvas below, outline then paint a detailed picture of a friend.
Cut around the edges of the frame and you will have a picture worthy of hanging!

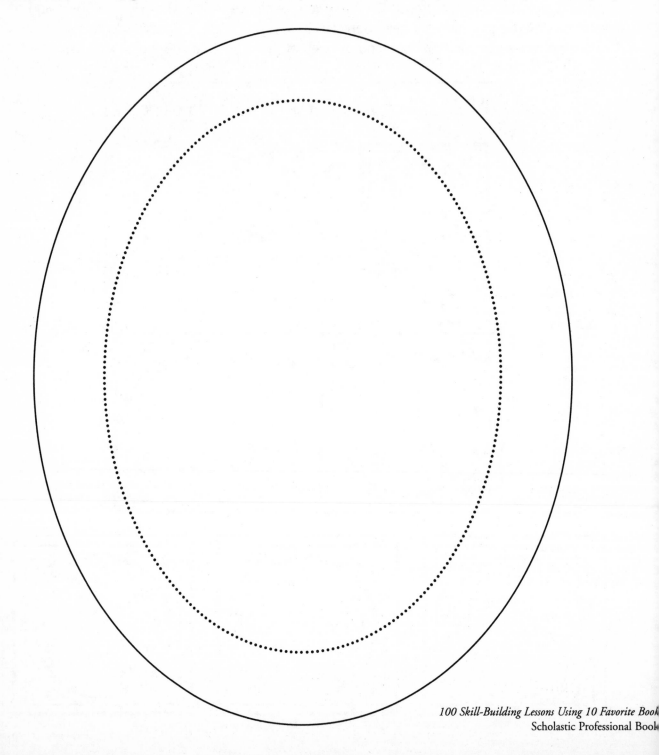

100 Skill-Building Lessons Using 10 Favorite Book
Scholastic Professional Book

Name _____ Date _____

Puppy School

Puppy Problems

Kathy and Louise are taking Golden Silverwind to puppy school. He is learning how to sit, stay, come when called, and wait. The teacher asks that the girls fill out a weekly practice schedule to ensure that Golden Silverwind gets into a good practice routine. Sometimes the girls forget to fill out the chart. Please help the girls figure out how many minutes they should have worked on the unmarked days below in order to have trained Golden Silverwind a total of 60 minutes each week. The totals must add up to 60 minutes each week.

	Week 1	Week 2	Week 3	Week 4	Week 5
Monday	5	15	10	10	—
Tuesday	5	7	11	—	—
Wednesday	10	—	—	—	0
Thursday	10	—	14	—	—
Friday	—	13	—	—	—
Saturday	6	5	5	20	24
Sunday	4	0	—	5	—
Total Minutes	**60**	**60**	**60**	**60**	**60**

Use the space below for adding numbers from the above chart.

Puppy Problems — New Toys

Kathy and Louise have saved $8.00 to buy Golden Silverwind some puppy toys and one box of treats from the pet store. Look at the toys pictured below and the price of each. Help the girls decide what they could buy for Golden Silverwind and still have $1.50 left over to buy him a box of dog treats as rewards for his training. Their mothers have told the girls to think about saving some change to put toward his next box of dog treats. Think of at least 4 possible ways for the girls to spend their money.

Toys	Option 1	Option 2	Option 3	Option 4
Tennis Balls $0.50 each	2 for $1.00			
Treat Teaser $5.00				
Tug Rope $3.50	$3.50			
Large Ball $2.29				
Stuffed Kitty $1.50	$1.50			
Box of Treats	$1.50	$1.50	$1.50	$1.50
Total	$7.50			
Change	$0.50			

Use the space below for adding the prices of the toys and treats above.

100 Skill-Building Lessons Using 10 Favorite Books   Scholastic Professional Books

Chapter Nine

There Are Secrets All Around Us

LESSONS 81 TO 90

Night Tree
by Eve Bunting

Mini-Lessons Across the Curriculum

Language Arts

Book Sense	*Using sensory details*
The Five Senses	*Practicing using sensory details*
Traditions	*Writing stories with reflective endings*
Younger Sisters (and Brothers) Are Like That	*A character study of Nina*

Math & Science

How Many Days Until...	*Calendar math activities*
School Tree	*Decorating a tree with food for animals*
Animals in Winter	*Discovering how animals prepare for winter*
Nature Walk	*Identifying animal signs*

Community

Afternoon Gathering	*Community building*

Art

A Traditions Quilt	*Making a keepsake quilt*

Book Sense

GOAL *Using Sensory Details*

 "'Here's our tree,' Dad says. It has been our tree forever and ever. We walk around it, touching it. 'It's grown since last year,' I say. Mom puts her hand on my shoulder. 'So have you.' 'So have I,' Nina says. Nina hates to be left out. An owl hoots, deep in the darkness. There are secrets all around us. "

~*Night Tree* by Eve Bunting, pp. 12–14.

One morning eight years ago, my friend and fellow teacher, Jodi Kamin, sent her copy of *Night Tree* to my classroom by way of a student messenger. A yellow sticky note on the front cover ordered "You MUST read this book. You will love it!" She was right. After reading it on the spot, as I am inclined to do when a brand new book by one of my favorite authors is placed in my hands, I instantly deemed *Night Tree* a favorite.

That afternoon for read-aloud, I shared *Night Tree* with my first and second graders. We marveled at Eve Bunting's word choice and how her language made us feel warm and cozy even in our brightly lit, slightly chilly classroom. We reread favorite passages and then talked about our own family traditions. Although it was only the beginning of November, my students and I couldn't wait for the holidays; we vowed to make a "night tree" of our own with our families and reread the book throughout the school year—anytime we felt we needed a little Christmas, so to speak.

I knew I would never be able to use this book strictly as a holiday read-aloud. I wanted to use Eve Bunting's ability to evoke emotions with words to inspire my beginning writers to do the same. Young children often are able to say more complex sentences than they feel challenged to write, and I thought her work would spur them on.

I decided to help students focus on the words Eve Bunting chooses that make us want to grab a cup of hot chocolate and venture out into the "bright Christmas streets where the dark and quiet begins" to search for a night tree of our own. What does Eve Bunting do to help her readers feel, see, hear, smell, and perhaps even taste the book *Night Tree*? What techniques can we borrow from this gifted author to help us make lasting impressions in the stories we write?

The mini-lesson that follows encourages students to stretch themselves and include all five senses when writing. I take five pieces of chart paper and label the first one with "Words We Can See," the others with "Words We Can Hear," "Words We Can Smell," "Words We Can Feel" and "Words We Can Taste" respectively. I hang the charts near our gathering space. To make the read-aloud memorable, I invite students to sit on a wool blanket placed on the floor. I warm my hands around a cup of hot chocolate as I wait for students to join me for a rereading of one of our beloved books—*Night Tree*.

Teaching Tip

The sentences taken from *Night Tree* in the following mini-lesson are too long to record during the lesson. I write the beginning words of each sentence as a student suggests it and leave an adequate amount of space for writing the rest of the sentence after the lesson, perhaps after school that day. This allows us to read the completed sentences the day following the mini-lesson without breaking the flow of the lesson or causing too much restlessness among the students.

Sam: The blanket and your cup of coffee make me think we're out in the cold—just like *Night Tree*!

Mrs. L.: I thought the blanket might make our mini-lesson based on *Night Tree* a little more fun.

Molly: Will you read it again?

Mrs. L.: I'm going to read parts of *Night Tree* for our writers' workshop meeting time. Eve Bunting is an expert on writing words to describe the five senses. On the charts, I've written words that describe the five senses—

Class: Seeing, smelling, hearing, feeling, and tasting.

Mrs. L.: Right. Can you recall any parts of *Night Tree* where you could see, smell, hear, feel, or taste what was happening in the story?

Matthew: The part where they warm their hands on the cup. It's after the tree is decorated.

Mrs. L.: I'll find that part.

Samantha: There it is. The page where they are spreading the blanket on the ground.

Mrs. L.: Listen to the words Eve Bunting used to help us feel his part:

I take off my gloves and toast my hands around my warm cup.

Ben: That makes my hands feel warm, too, just hearing the words.

Mrs. L.: Then I would say Eve Bunting did an excellent job of helping you feel what the little boy in the story was feeling. I think one particular word makes this sentence extra-special.

David: I like the word *toast*. Like toasting bread in the toaster.

Elizabeth: Except he is toasting his hands on his cup, sort of.

Mrs. L.: *Toast* is the word I was thinking of. What would you think of this sentence if she had written, *I take off my gloves and warm my hands around my cup?*

Courtney: It would still be good, but *toasting hands* is better.

Mrs. L.: I'll write this sentence on the "Words We Can Feel" chart. Tell me about another sentence from the story that helped you use your senses to understand what was happening in the story. I'll flip through the pages to spark your memories.

Stephanie: Read page one again for us.

Mrs. L.: Sure.

On the night before Christmas we always go to find our tree. We bundle up so we're warm. Nina is already wearing her boots that are too big for her. She has been wearing them all day—

Eric: I can feel how warm they are all bundled up in the car.

Mrs. L.: That feeling when you're dressed in layers to be outside but being inside the car makes you feel too warm?

Eric: Yes!

Mrs. L.: I think there is a word or two in this sentence that helps us feel warm.

Matthew: Bundle up.

Mrs. L.: Bundled has a warm and cozy sound to it. Tell me about Nina on page one.

Jack: She's excited!

Mrs. L.: How excited?

Jack: So excited she's been wearing her boots all day because she wants to be ready to go when the time finally comes.

Hannah: And they didn't go until night so she had to be excited in her boots all day long.

Stephanie: I bet her feet were hot!

Tyler: And the boots were too big for her so they probably weren't that comfortable.

Mrs. L.: Smile if you have ever felt this excited about something. Eve Bunting didn't write the words, Nina is excited. She helped you feel this by painting a picture of Nina wearing her boots around the house all day. Since we can feel Nina's excitement, I'll write this sentence on our chart under feelings, too. It's not the kind of feeling where you can touch something; it's the kind of feelings you have inside. Listen as I read part of the next page.

Nina is almost asleep in Mom's lap when we stop.

"Are we there?" I ask, and Dad says "Yes" and rolls down the windows so we can smell the tree smell.

Anna: I can smell the trees, too. They are pine trees I think.

Alex: I love the smell of pine trees.

Hannah: Me, too. You should write that down under smelling.

Mrs. L.: Good thinking. I'll write, Dad says 'Yes' and rolls down the window so we can smell the tree smell.

Emma: Read the next page, please.

Mrs. L.: Sure:

> This is called Luke's Forest, but Dad says it's not really a forest, just a nice forgotten place where our town ends. Dad goes first on the path between the trees, carrying our box and the big red lantern.
>
> Mom and Nina go next, holding hands. I come last, with the blanket.

Lauren: I can see them walking toward the tree even without the picture.

Mrs. L.: Eve Bunting included a lot of details to help you see this, didn't she? She could have just written, *We walked toward our tree.*

Alex: That wouldn't have been as good.

Mrs. L.: Tell me about that.

Alex: I like hearing how Nina and Mom hold hands and the boy has the blanket.

Jack: And how Dad goes first since he's got the lantern.

David: You could write that sentence under seeing.

Mrs. L.: Good idea. I like how Dad says it's not really a forest, but *just a nice forgotten place where our town ends.* You can imagine stores and the bright Christmas streets on the edge of Luke's Forest. I suppose we could include all of Eve Bunting's sentences on our chart, if we really thought about them.

Ben: She is an expert!

Mrs. L.: I agree. She certainly helps her readers use their senses while reading her books, which is probably why she is one of my favorite authors. Let's think of something that happened in the story that made us use our sense of hearing.

Emma: When they were singing "Old MacDonald."

We peruse a few more pages, identifying a few more sentences to add to our list. I make sure we find sentences for each sense.

Mrs. L.: I'm sure Eve Bunting works hard to make her words just right so that her readers can see what she sees, smell what she smells, and so on. Readers may not be there to smell the trees, or hear the owl hooting deep in the darkness, but the words she uses help us be a part of these experiences. Now let's see what kinds of words you can include in your stories to help your audience see, hear, smell, and feel what is happening in your stories.

Using Our Five Senses to Read Night Tree

Sentences We Can See

- There are oaks growing here and alder and maples that are bare now and white in the moonshine.
- Dad goes first on the path between the trees, carrying our box and the big red lantern. Mom and Nina go next, holding hands. I come last with the blanket.
- The sky is spattered with stars, and the moon, big as a basketball, slides in and out between the treetops.
- A deer is watching us. I see the brightness of its eyes.
- Our tree has folded itself into the darkness, but I think I can see it still, stars caught in its branches and the moon swinging lopsided on top.
- Maybe a fox has come, stepping high on its thin, sharp paws, and they're all there together, singing their own Christmas songs on Christmas Day around our tree.

Sentences We Can Hear

- An owl hoots deep in the darkness. There are secrets all around us.
- We sing fast because there are a lot of verses and it's getting colder.
- Dad turns off the lantern and we stay quiet, hoping some of the little animals will come while we're here, hoping the deer will come back. But it doesn't.
- Later, in bed, I think about our tree, and sometimes, next day, when the aunts and the uncles and the cousins are at our house and it's noisy and happy, I let my mind go back to Luke's Forest.

Sentences We Can Smell

- "Are we there?" I ask, and Dad says "Yes" and rolls down the windows so we can smell the tree smell.

Sentences We Can Feel

- I take off my gloves and toast my hands around my warm cup.
- Nina is already wearing her boots that are too big for her. She has been wearing them all day.
- She hops up and down and right out of one of her boots.
- It's so cold my breath hurts.
- It has been our tree forever and ever. We walk around it, touching it.

Sentences We Can Taste

- We've brought apples and tangerines with strings on them, and we hang them from the branches. She has brought a thermos of hot chocolate.

Independent Practice

The Five Senses: Practicing Using Sensory Details

Mrs. L.: Now that you've had a chance to see how an expert uses words to make stories come alive with the five senses, it's time for you to give this a try in your own writing. First, think about a tradition in your family.

Lauren: We always rake leaves on Saturdays in the fall and drink apple cider.

Stephanie: We make big breakfasts together on Saturdays.

Mrs. L.: Both of these traditions would make wonderful stories and could be described using the five senses—I can hear you crunching in the leaves as you rake them, Lauren. I'm sure I'll be able to smell your breakfast cooking if you write what it is, Stephanie.

Stephanie: It's either eggs, pancakes, or waffles. We vote on it the night before.

Mrs. L.: What a great way to start a weekend. Let's help Stephanie write a sentence to describe breakfast. Everyone close your eyes and imagine your house on a Saturday morning when breakfast is cooking. What do you hear, smell, taste, feel, and see?

Madison: It smells like coffee every morning in our house.

Mrs. L.: Mine does, too. I love to wake up and smell coffee waiting for me!

Matthew: I love to hear bacon cooking at our house.

Mrs. L.: What does it sound like?

Matthew: It makes a 'chshhhs' sound.

Lauren: It's sizzling!

Matthew: She could write "Chshshshs. The sound of sizzling bacon wakes me every Saturday morning."

Stephanie: "And the smell of coffee dripping in the pot."

Mrs. L.: You're off to a good start at using the five senses in writing. For sharing time today, I'll ask you to share a favorite sentence you have written that uses one of the five senses.

During sharing time, many of the students were surprised by their accomplishments. This technique, borrowed from an expert author, gave students confidence and encouragement in their writing efforts as well as a more tangible way for their audience to experience the events taking place in stories shared.

Favorite Sentences Using the Five Senses

- My boots crunched in the snow as I walked to the bird feeder.
- I walked in the door and smelled the cookies Mom made just for me.
- My cat licked my hand with her scratchy tongue.
- The snow was wet and my feet were cold even though I had on three pairs of socks.
- The soup was hot and a little spicy at first.

8 More Book-Based Lessons

Traditions: Writing Stories With Reflective Endings

Have students get more inspiration from *Night Tree* by writing a story that describes a celebrated family tradition. Students can use the sentences from the independent follow-up lesson to get started and then write a story describing their family tradition. Encourage students to write a reflective ending to their stories. Discuss the last two pages of *Night Tree* to illustrate how the boy lies in bed imagining the animals having Christmas dinner around his tree:

> Later, in bed, I think about our tree, and sometimes, next day, when the aunts and the uncles and the cousins are at our house and it's noisy and happy, I let my mind go back to Luke's Forest.
>
> I think of the birds having Christmas dinner and the squirrels and the opossums and the raccoons and the skunks.

> When I'm older, I will always remember Saturday breakfasts with my brother and Mom and Dad and how we started our weekend with scrambled eggs and sausage.

▲ *One Student's Reflective Ending.*

Afternoon Gathering: Community Building

Make a Friday afternoon in winter extra-special with this community-building activity *Night Tree* style. Buy ready-made popcorn (or pop it together) and bring an electric hot-pot for boiling water to make instant hot chocolate. Have students bundle up, if necessary, and take them outside to sit near your "School Tree." While students enjoy popcorn and hot chocolate, they can take turns sharing stories based on family traditions of their own. If your class has made a traditions quilt (see page 142), this is a nice time to unveil the finished product. For added fun, invite another class to join you for this special gathering of friends. Offer a brief explanation of your *Night Tree* projects to your guests, of course!

Younger Sisters (and Brothers) Are Like That: A Character Study of Nina

Each time I read *Night Tree* at least one older sibling of the class comments "my little sister (or brother) is just like Nina." Take the opportunity presented in this story to have your students do a character study of Nina. Invite students to recall sentences from the story that describe Nina, and record inferences that can be made about Nina based on her actions in *Night Tree*:

Things We Know About Nina

- ☼ She doesn't like to be left out.
- ☼ She likes to sing "Old MacDonald Had a Farm."
- ☼ She gets excited a lot—wears boots all day, hops up and down and out of her boot.
- ☼ Gets caught up in excitement.
- ☼ Young—she almost falls asleep in the truck, always wants to do things her way (putting popcorn chain on), gets tired so dad wraps her in the blanket and carries her.
- ☼ She is shy like the deer who won't come back.

Next have students make predictions about how Nina would behave if placed in situations such as those listed below. Ideas should be supported by her actions in *Night Tree*. For example, since Nina wanted to be the first one to put on the popcorn chain, she probably will want to go first when playing a game with her brother. Likewise, she will probably fall asleep on the couch while staying up late to watch a holiday show since she fell asleep in the truck on the way home from decorating the *Night Tree*.

How Would Nina Behave When:

- ☼ Having a friend over to play
- ☼ Playing a new game with her brother
- ☼ Discovering her brother is invited to a special event with a friend—she's too young to go
- ☼ Seeing a clown at a birthday party
- ☼ Staying up late with family to watch a special holiday show

How Many Days Until...: Calendar Math Activities

Are we there yet? How many days until Christmas? My birthday? Time is a difficult concept for young children to grasp, and waiting for special days to arrive seems to take forever. Using a calendar to help students visualize how far away a special day is can ease the waiting and help students learn to appreciate the concept of days and months.

Begin each new month by marking special occasions to look forward to on a bulletin board sized calendar with sticky notes or a pencil. Class birthdays, special school events, and holidays are some days to highlight. As part of your morning routine, pose questions to students to help them see how the calendar is set up and how many days or weeks until special days arrive. Be sure to ask students to demonstrate how they arrived at particular answers to illustrate that there is more than one way to solve a problem.

Calendar Questions

- ☼ The first Friday of this month is...The second Tuesday of this month is...
- ☼ How many days until Ben's birthday on the 18?
- ☼ How many days apart are Alex and Stephanie's birthdays?
- ☼ Two weeks from yesterday will be...

Help students discover the various number patterns used on the calendar by examining the numbers arranged on the calendar's grid (see list at right).

To get all students involved in this daily calendar time, make copies of the blank calendar found on page 145 and have students number the calendar and fill in the special days highlighted on the bulletin board calendar as you write on the class bulletin board calendar.

Discovering Patterns

- ☼ Add 1 as you go from left to right
- ☼ Add 7 as you go horizontally down a row of numbers
- ☼ Add 8 diagonally from left to right
- ☼ Add 6 diagonally from right to left

◀ *A Calendar for April*

School Tree: Decorating a Tree With Food for Animals

Ask students to work together to decorate a "School Tree" for the animals in your school neighborhood to enjoy. Set up four different tree-decorating stations with ideas out of the pages of *Night Tree*, and invite students to take turns making treats to decorate a tree on school property. If possible, you may wish to adopt a tree that can be viewed from your classroom (unless this will be too disruptive every time a critter comes to the tree for a snack).

Ask parents to donate the items needed for each station and perhaps to volunteer on the day students work at the "School Tree Stations." You may wish to have students work at one center a day for a week, or set up the centers for students to use during their free time, or set aside one hour or more where small groups rotate to each of the project areas. As a kick-off to the "Afternoon Gathering," decorate your School Tree and then enjoy hot chocolate and popcorn while students share Traditions Stories.

STATION #1 • Honey Apples

Though a bit sticky, this center is a favorite for students! First, thread heavy cord through the tops of apples using blunt darning needles. Make loops in the cords for hanging. Next, dip apples in bowls of honey and roll them in plates filled with bird or sunflower seeds. Place the honey apples in empty soda cases until it is time to hang them on the School Tree.

STATION #2 • Popcorn Strings

Pop a fresh batch of popcorn (hot air or microwave without butter for less mess) and be sure to allow for a few nibbles by hard working students! Supply blunt (but smaller sized) darning needles pre-threaded with string for students to make individual chains. The chains could be connected into one chain or left individually to hang around the tree's width.

STATION #3
Apples and Tangerines

Students thread blunt darning needles with heavy cord or string and loop through apples and tangerines. Knot loop at the top and the treats are ready to be hung from the School Tree!

STATION #4
Shelled Nuts and Bread Crumbs

At this station, students work on shelling various nuts and crumbling bread to scatter on the ground "for the little creatures who can't climb very well." Provide assorted nuts and nut crackers for students to use (volunteers can bring these in from home). Fill one coffee can with the shelled nuts and another with bread crumbs, which the students crumble at the center as well.

A Traditions Quilt: Making a Keepsake Quilt

One of my favorite pages of *Night Tree* is the next to the last page where the little boy is lying in bed, reflecting upon the animals back at Luke's Forest. Each time I read this page, at least one student notices the quilt tucked carefully over the boy, depicting his family's "Night Tree." We surmise that the little boy and his mother worked together to create this special quilt and marvel at the detail that Ted Rand included to help readers understand just how special the tree is to this family.

Help your students create a memorable quilt to display in the classroom. First, enlist the help of parents in donating muslin fabric or solid color scraps so that each student has one 7 x 7 inch square of fabric (or any size you wish). As a class, select a theme for the quilt. The quilt may relate to a unit of study (such as our pioneer quilt shown on page 143), depict favorite memories of the school year, fond family traditions, or another topic of your choice.

Give students a piece of 7 x 7 inch paper to plan their design in pencil before giving them "good" quilt paper. Students draw their "good copy" designs on a 7 x 7 inch piece of paper (newsprint or copy paper works well), using fabric crayons (available in craft sections of most department stores). Include a square with the name or theme of the quilt and the year the quilt was made for future reference.

It is helpful to have one or more parent volunteers complete the next three quilt-making steps at home. One parent volunteer transfers each individual design from the paper onto individual muslin fabric squares using a hot iron. Another parent volunteer sews the squares together on a sewing machine.

A precious keepsake from my first year of teaching, this quilt was made for me while I was out sick with chicken pox.

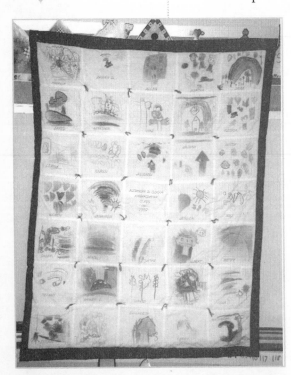

Occasionally, two parents work together on this step, as some planning is needed to make the quilt symmetrical (each year I find I have at least one eager parent handy with a sewing machine). A fabric border can be attached to the front of the quilt (see sample at left). Finally, the front pieces are attached to a quilted backing (available at fabric stores or fabric departments of some department stores).

The quilt is then returned to the classroom for the students' finishing touch. Have students attach yarn knots to the quilt, using a matching color of yarn. Thread large darning needles with yarn, bring the yarn though both layers of fabric from the top of the quilt and pop back up through both layers underneath; then tie in a knot. The knots are usually added between each of the corners of the fabric pieces. The yarn knots, though optional, give the quilt a more complete look and give students a sense of assisting in the quilt-making process. With a fabric marker, include students' names before displaying the finished quilt on the wall of the classroom.

Quilt-Making Tips

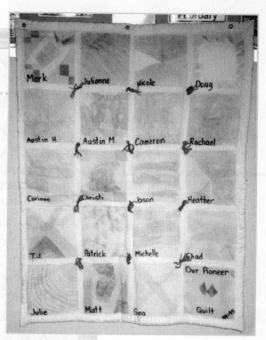

☀ Do not be intimidated by this activity! The most time-consuming part is lining up the parent volunteers to assist with piecing the quilt together. The results are well worth the effort! The first keepsake quilt you see at left, done completely by a parent volunteer, gave me the inspiration and direction to try this activity. Each quilt ensures a keepsake of every class I teach.

☀ You can adjust the size of the square to accommodate the number of students you have to make a quilt that is "symmetrical"—23 students works nicely with 6 rows of 4 squares including the name and date square, but 21 students makes for some careful planning!

☀ Directions for this process are outlined on the back of the box of fabric crayons—remind students to press hard when drawing with the crayons so that the image transfers better.

☀ Have students put all other crayons away prior to using the fabric crayons so they do not confuse "school crayons" with fabric crayons or the parent volunteer will have a messy iron!

Our Pioneer Quilt 94–95

Animals in Winter: Discovering How Animals Prepare for Winter

Give students a research project to help them identify the special preparations animals make for winter. Have students work alone or with a partner to choose an animal from the last page of *Night Tree* to research. On this page, creatures such as owls, hawks, raccoons, skunks, fox, beaver, rabbits, porcupines, opossums, otters, doves, deer, crows, cardinals, blue jays, squirrels, mice, and bears are enjoying the treats of the *Night Tree* on Christmas day.

Provide time for pairs of students to locate books at the library (or use the Internet) to assist them in identifying what animals do to prepare for a long winter. Use the "Animals in Winter Fact Sheet" on page 146 to help students locate and record such information.

I usually ask that students share a photo of their animal from a book, if possible. Allow time for students to share the results of their research or to create an Animals in Winter bulletin board where they can display their fact-finding sheets for others to view and learn about the habits of different animals in winter.

Nature Walk: Identifying Animal Signs

My classroom is in a rural setting, with trees and cornfields nearby, so occasionally interesting creatures visit us on the playground. One morning we spied an owl perched in a tree, and on another day a hawk flew overhead during recess. In years past, a white horse grazed on the farm bordering our school. Walking the perimeter of our school property can provide my students with sightings of these and other interesting animals. So, after reading *Night Tree*, we take a quiet nature walk, equipped with paper and pencils on clipboards.

As the students quietly walk, they look for signs of animals—footprints, bits of chewed acorns, rubbings on trees, or even the animals themselves: squirrels or birds, for example. Students make notes of these findings. Back in the classroom, they draw pictures to illustrate their findings, labeling each one.

If your classroom is not in this type of rural setting, take a nature walk of a different nature! Paint a picture with words of what you see on an imaginary nature walk, describing for students the animals and signs of animals described above. You might describe a chipmunk by saying, "What is this I see? A small brown animal, about the length of a pencil. He has a dark stripe down his back and tail, and his cheeks are filled with nuts."

Students can add descriptions of their own before drawing a picture of their nature walk upon "returning" to the classroom.

More Books by Eve Bunting

The Blue and the Gray (Scholastic Press, 1996)

Dandelions (Harcourt Brace & Company, 1995)

Dreaming of America—An Ellis Island Story (Troll BridgeWater Books, 2000)

The Day the Whale Came (Harcourt Brace & Company, 1998)

Fly Away Home (Clarion Books, 1991)

The Mother's Day Mice (Clarion Books, 1986)

A Picnic in October (Harcourt Brace & Company, 1999)

Someday a Tree (Clarion Books, 1993)

St. Patrick's Day in the Morning (Clarion Books, 1980)

Train to Somewhere (Clarion Books, 1996)

The Valentine Bears (Clarion Books, 1983)

The Wednesday Surprise (Clarion Books, 1989)

Name _____ Date _____

This is my calendar for the month of

_____

Sunday	Monday	Tuesday	Wednesday	Thursday	Friday	Saturday

100 Skill-Building Lessons Using 10 Favorite Books   Scholastic Professional Books

Name _____ Date _____

 # Animals in Winter Fact Sheet

Here are three physical characteristics of my animal:

(1) _____

(2) _____

(3) _____

Some of my animal's favorite foods are _____

_____.

To get ready for a long winter, my animal

_____

_____.

My animal lives in _____.

Two of my animal's enemies are _____

and _____.

I think my animal is special because _____

_____.

Here is a list of the book(s) I used to help gather this information: _____

_____

I have attached a picture of my animal in winter.

100 Skill-Building Lessons Using 10 Favorite Books   Scholastic Professional Books

Chapter Ten

A Dog for a Week

LESSONS 91 TO 100

*The Bookshop Dog
by Cynthia Rylant*

Mini-Lessons Across the Curriculum

Language Arts

Martha Jane for a Week	*Making story outlines*
On Our Own	*Practicing making story outlines*
Martha Jane Loved Hawaii	*Writing unique endings*
A Bookshop Is a Shop with Books	*Identifying compound words*
Thank You, Get Well, Happy Wedding, and More!	*Letter-writing activities*

Math & Science

Two Dogs and Two Cats	*Graphing activities*
Martha Jane's Bakery	*Making dog treats for charity*

Community

Love Your Pet	*Making posters to encourage responsible pet ownership*
Dog Days	*Organizing school visits from dogs*
Little Things Mean a Lot	*Encouraging good deeds*

Martha Jane for a Week

GOAL *Making Story Outlines*

> "A man in a green coat walked through the crowd. He had a Beefy Bone in his hand. He knelt down beside Martha Jane and stroked her smooth head and kissed her warm white face and told her what an angel dog she was. At the sound of his voice, everyone grew quiet and only Martha Jane's crunchings could be heard. Martha Jane had made her choice."
>
> ~*The Bookshop Dog*
> by Cynthia Rylant, pp. 27.

You don't have to be a dog lover to enjoy this book. Students love to hear how customers at the bookshop call and ask for Martha Jane's advice, not knowing the woman named the store after her dog, Martha Jane. They giggle when the children at the Bookshop "swatted each other with their bags of kibble." And they especially like the ending when Martha Jane gets to go on a honeymoon to Hawaii. We had just finished reading this book at about the time I planned to introduce story outlining to my students. The clear sequence of events leading up to a happy conclusion makes *The Bookshop Dog* a perfect story for such a lesson. The conflict of the story is clear: Everyone loves Martha Jane so much that when she needs a sitter, they all want to volunteer! Who will she choose?

I use story outlining to evaluate reading comprehension. Students read a story independently and then use a simple story outline to record the main characters, setting, and main events in the beginning, middle, and end of the story. Being able to label the various parts of the story helps students understand the importance of reading for understanding, not simply reading words on a page. We discuss how sometimes even the most careful readers read too quickly to grasp the meaning of a particular page. At these times, rereading for understanding is crucial, for without meaning, words are nothing more than letters on a page.

Before I have students outline a story independently, we outline one together to ensure that everyone understands the story-outlining process. In the lesson that follows, Martha Jane, the Bookshop Dog, lends a paw to help students read for understanding and to give them practice in outlining a story.

To prepare for this lesson, I record the words from the first page of *The Bookshop Dog* in scrambled order onto a chart. On the second sheet of the chart, I record the page as it appears in the book:

> Once there was a woman who loved her dog so much that she could hardly bear to be away from her. The woman took her dog to the park. She took her to the market.

Next, I tape a large sheet of butcher paper on the board, long ways from left to right, near our gathering space. I copy the headings (as shown at right) on the paper leaving ample space for recording student ideas.

Teaching Tip

Using butcher paper or the overhead rather than the board itself ensures that the story outline can be saved for future reference rather than erased when the board space is needed later in the day.

Title:
Author:
Characters:
Setting:
☼ Beginning   ☼ Middle   ☼ Ending

Mrs. L.:	I've copied the words from the first page of *The Bookshop Dog* onto this piece of chart paper. Would you read them, please.

> Once woman park there took market dog the hardly away from was took bear dog the to could a The She to her her her so woman to be who she that loved her much

Ben:	That's not the first page of *The Bookshop Dog*.
Mrs. L.:	Yes, these are the words from the first page.
Madison:	They don't make sense.
Mrs. L.:	I agree. These are the words from the first page, but I wasn't careful to copy them in the right order. Actually, I did this on purpose because I wanted to help you see how important it is to be careful when you read. Cynthia Rylant is trying to tell us a story. Without reading carefully, her story is just words on a page. Words without meaning attached won't make sense. When you are reading, you need to think about what is being read so that you understand what the author wanted to tell you. This is called *comprehending*, or understanding what you are reading. It is wonderful to be able to read any word in front of us, but it is even more important to understand what that word means when it's put together with others in a sentence.
Stephanie:	Sometimes I have to reread a page if my mind starts thinking of something else.
Matthew:	Me, too.

Mrs. L.:	Rereading when something doesn't make sense is something all good readers do. That's part of being a careful reader. Here are the words from page one as Cynthia Rylant wrote them. Please read along silently as I read aloud:

Once there was a woman who loved her dog so much that she could hardly bear to be away from her. The woman took her dog to the park. She took her to the market.

Mrs. L.:	Tell me in your own words what Cynthia Rylant wants her readers to understand as they read this first page of *The Bookshop Dog*.
Collin:	That she loves her dog a lot.
Eric:	Really a lot!
Molly:	So much that she has to take her everywhere she goes—
Tyler:	Like the park and the market.
Mrs. L.:	You are wonderful readers and listeners! You comprehended the first page very well. Today we are going to make a story outline of *The Bookshop Dog*. A story outline gives the main events or ideas in the story. When we finish recording our ideas on the outline, we should be able to retell the story of *The Bookshop Dog* by looking at our outline. Let's begin filling in the story outline for *The Bookshop Dog*.
Jack:	We know the title and the author.
Mrs. L.:	I'll write *The Bookshop Dog* by Cynthia Rylant.
Emma:	Next, we write the characters. Martha Jane should be first since she is The Bookshop Dog.
Madison:	And then her owner.
Mrs. L.:	Do we know her name?
Lauren:	No, she is "the woman." Write the "big man in the green coat," too.
Mrs. L.:	Good thinking.
Collin:	There are customers in the story. The people buying books.
Samantha:	But they weren't really important. They didn't do anything in the story.
David:	You could include the band director and the policeman. They taught Martha Jane things like singing and how to get the mail out of the mailbox.
Matthew:	The band director and the postman and the policeman are more important than the other customers who maybe just called on the phone to get Martha Jane's advice.
Mrs. L.:	Under characters I have Martha Jane, the woman, the big man in the green coat, the band director, the policeman and the postman. Anyone else?
Molly:	What about the children who hit each other over the head with bags of dog treats?
Mrs. L.:	I'll list "children," too. Now tell me about the setting of this story. There are two parts to every setting.
Lauren:	Time and place. It's definitely in the present day. The people are dressed like we would dress.

Jack:	And there are cars and stores, too.
Mrs. L.:	Smile if you agree that I should write "present day" as the time of the setting. (I see lots of smiles.) Present day it is. What about the place?
Alex:	The bookshop.
Sam:	No, sometimes the story is not in the bookshop. They go to the park on the first page.
Matthew:	And Hawaii on the last page!
Alex:	But the story is mostly in the bookshop.
Mrs. L.:	Since most of the story takes place in the bookshop, it is acceptable to write the setting as present day in a bookshop. A "present day town" would be fine, as well. What's next on our outline?
David:	The "beginning."
Mrs. L.:	This is where we write the main events that took place at the beginning of the story. The beginning is usually where we meet the main characters. The beginning leads us to the middle of the story where the—
Lauren:	Problem happens.
Madison:	The conflict.
Mrs. L.:	Good remembering. Tell me about the beginning of *The Bookshop Dog*.
Molly:	The beginning is where we find out how much the woman loves Martha Jane—so much that she takes her everywhere with her.
Collin:	To the dentist, the market, the park.
David:	And to work.
Eric:	Everyone in the whole town loves Martha Jane because she is so sweet and nice.
Mrs. L.:	Good work! Now tell me about the middle of the story.
Matthew:	That's where the problem happens. The woman becomes sick and finds out she needs to go to the hospital. She isn't allowed to take Martha Jane with her. Everyone wants Martha Jane for a week.
Lauren:	The problem is who will take care of Martha Jane.
Mrs. L.:	Or, who will Martha Jane pick to take care of her!
Lauren:	The band director and the policeman and the post man and the children all start fighting while Martha Jane and the big man in the green coat are talking and eating beefy bones.
Mrs. L.:	Is this the ending?
Anna:	Not yet. The ending is when the man takes such good care of Martha Jane that the woman gets back from the hospital and marries him.
Matthew:	The ending is that they all had a good time on the honeymoon in Hawaii.
Mrs. L.:	I'll include both of these ideas as part of the ending. You have done an excellent job of remembering this story. Let's read our outline to make sure we didn't forget anything:

TITLE:	*The Bookshop Dog*
AUTHOR:	Cynthia Rylant
CHARACTERS:	Martha Jane, the woman, the big man in the green coat, postman, policeman, band director, children
SETTING:	Present day in a bookshop

BEGINNING	MIDDLE	ENDING
A woman loved her dog so much, she took her everywhere with her.	The woman gets ill and has to go to the hospital.	Martha Jane chooses the man in the green coat to take care of her.
☼ to the park ☼ to the dentist ☼ to work	Martha Jane cannot go to the hospital.	He takes such good care of Martha Jane and the bookshop, the woman marries the man.
Everyone loved Martha Jane.	Who will take care of Martha Jane?	The woman, the man in the green coat, and Martha Jane have a great time on the honeymoon in Hawaii!
	The postman, policeman, band director, and the children all begin fighting over Martha Jane.	

Mrs. L.: You have done a great job of outlining this story. The next time you read a book by yourself, think about the parts of this outline. If you have read the story carefully and understand what you have read, you should be able to recall these parts of the story. Remember, the most important part of reading is understanding what the words mean when they are put together.

◀ *Working on Story Outlines*

Independent Practice

On Our Own:
Practicing Making Story Outlines

Mrs. L.: I'm going to give you a chance to make your own story outline of *The Bookshop Dog* so that you can share it at home. Fill in the information at the very top. Next, illustrate what happened in the beginning, middle, and ending of *The Bookshop Dog*.

Ben: Do we write the words from the chart, too?

Mrs. L.: Feel free to label each part with any words that will help you tell about your picture. A copy of *The Bookshop Dog* is here for you to share for help with your illustrations, if needed.

I encourage students to make detailed illustrations and provide time for pairs of students to retell the story using finished outlines. When the time comes to complete an outline for a story read independently, allowing students to use illustrations takes the pressure off early sound spellers, who may become frustrated by the task but who did comprehend what was read. Since the outline is to check reading comprehension, not sound spelling, confer with students so they can tell about their outline, using their pictures for guidance. Most important, make sure the book to be read independently is at an appropriate reading level for students.

Use a rubric similar to the one at right with the books your students read independently.

Rubric for Story Outlining

5 Powerful
- Ideas included go beyond the story
- Main characters are included
- Setting with time or place or both
- 5 major events that go from beginning, middle, to end

4 Competent
- Main characters are included
- Setting with time or place or both
- 3 or more events that go from beginning to middle to end

3 Incomplete
- Only one character
- No setting or incorrect setting
- Events not in order
- Some parts copied from book (if written words used)

2 Undeveloped
- Events not in order
- Only 1–2 events included

1 No Response

8 More Book-Based Lessons

Extra-Special Ending Sentences

Molly: Sally would always remember the birthday party.

Jack: Frog never ate too many flies for breakfast again.

Collin: Eddie loved Alaska.

Stephanie: Victoria, Sam and Ruby were friends forever.

Tyler: And Max Cat saved a bite of cheese for Harry Mouse.

Martha Jane Loved Hawaii: Writing Unique Endings

The last sentence from *The Bookshop Dog*, where Martha Jane is shown on a surfboard in Hawaii with a terrified look on her dog face as she rides a wave, always evokes a giggle from students. During a writers' workshop mini-lesson, we discuss how the story would be complete without this last page but how this final sentence—"Martha Jane loved Hawaii"—makes the ending extra special. The students agree the extra effort on Cynthia Rylant's part is greatly appreciated and add "just one more sentence" to the writers' workshop stories they are working on to make them extra special.

We begin a chart of special ending sentences from the students' writers' workshop stories (see samples at left), pay close attention to the ending sentences of books shared for read-aloud.

A Bookshop is a Shop with Books: Identifying Compound Words

The Bookshop Dog provides a number of opportunities to discuss compound words with your class. Use the list of compound words below from *The Bookshop Dog* and ask students to write definitions for the words. As you will see from our definition of "honeymoon" below, you will probably have a giggle or two as your students describe these compound words in their own words! Add other compound words to the list as you encounter them in reading and writing.

Compound Words We Know

bookshop a shop with books

salesman a man or woman who sells something like books (salesperson)

postman a man or woman who "posts" or delivers mail

policeman a man who polices or enforces laws

football a ball that is kicked with a foot

mailbox a box for mail

honeymoon Time right after a wedding when someone takes their honey to look at the moon

Thank You, Get Well, Happy Wedding, and More!: Letter-Writing Activities

Help your students practice letter writing using the characters from *The Bookshop Dog*. First introduce parts of a letter using the sample letter shown below from the children to Martha Jane. Then offer students letter-writing choices such as the following:

Write a letter...

☀ From Martha Jane to the woman telling about her week with the big man in the green coat
☀ From the woman to Martha Jane during her stay in the hospital
☀ From the man in the green coat to the woman at the hospital
☀ From the children to Martha Jane

Or make

☀ Wedding cards and notes to the man, woman, and Martha Jane
☀ Postcards from Hawaii to those back at the Bookshop
☀ Get well cards and notes to the woman from any of the characters
☀ Apology notes to Martha Jane and the Bookshop owner from those characters who got into arguments over Martha Jane

Bring in sample cards from home to help students design cards made from folded construction paper with a letter written on the inside. Notes can be written on "stationery"—writing paper on which students add a fancy border or corner design.

Encourage proofreading and perhaps both rough and final copies to help students understand the importance of writing legible letters that make sense.

Cover a shoe box with blue paper and cut a slit in the lid. Have students who finish early add designs for "Martha Jane's Bookshop Mailbox" as shown on page 31 of *The Bookshop Dog*. Finished letters to Martha Jane, the woman, and the big man in the green coat can be placed in the mailbox and shared with the class.

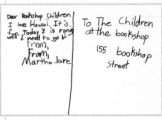

A Postcard from Hawaii

> November 3, 2000
>
> Dear Martha Jane,
>
> We are sorry about the argument we had over you. We hope we didn't upset you too much. It's just that we all wanted to take you home for a week while your mom was in the hospital. We hope you have a good time with the big man in the green coat. If you need more Beefy Bones, just let us know.
>
> Love,
> The Children from the Bookshop

Get Well Soon!

> Dear Woman,
>
> I hope you get well soon! I am having a fun time with the man in the green coat.
>
> Love,
> your dog
> Martha Jane

A Get-Well Card from Martha Jane

Little Things Mean a Lot: Encouraging Good Deeds

"The woman found that the big man in the green coat had painted her mailbox, dusted her shelves, washed her windows, and swept her floor. But most important, he had loved her dog."

Encourage similar acts of kindness from your students while brightening the days of school helpers. Have students make a cup of tea (using a hot pot in the classroom) and deliver it to the school secretary or principal. Groups of students could design cards thanking the custodians and cafeteria workers for their hard work. Work as a class to keep the classroom especially clean to make the custodians' job easier at the end of the day. Make a batch of "no-bake" or other cookies to share with these and other school helpers. Attach a note that says "We appreciate all you do to make our school a nice place to learn."

Take time to ask students to share kind acts they have performed at home for family and friends, as well. Consider giving a weekly Good Deed Award to encourage "community service" among your students.

Martha Jane's Bakery: Making Dog Treats for Charity

Martha Jane loved the Beefy Bones the big man in the green coat brought to her. Have your students make dog treats to take home for their special dogs, to save for the activity "Dog Days" below, and to donate to local animal charities. I found the recipe for "Snickerpoodles" while watching a show on the TV Food Network called "Three Dog Bakery." These treats come highly recommended by my two taste-testing Labrador Retrievers, Sydney and Jordan.

Make an overhead transparency of the recipe found on page 160, and set up a table filled with the necessary ingredients and cooking equipment. Students take turns reading and following the steps of the recipe with you. Then, working in small groups, they roll the balls of "Snickerpoodles" in cinnamon, press crossways with a fork, and place on a cookie sheet. I bake the treats at home that evening then bring them back to the school so the students can help me package the treats.

To make decorative tins for giving the treats away, students can cover potato chip or tennis ball cans (collected prior to the activity) with construction paper and decorate with dog designs. We include the recipe for owners who may wish to bake their own treats, as well as to provide a list of the ingredients for owners whose pets may have food allergies.

Dog Days: Organizing School Visits from Dogs

Students love to have their dogs come to school to meet their classmates. Send a letter home with student dog-owners inviting them to school (see our sample letter at right). In the letter, suggest a day and time for each dog's visit. I plan these visits at the end of the day to minimize disruptions to the rest of the day's schedule as visiting canines do have a way of exciting young children! Only "dogs who love children" are invited, and one dog a day works best. We are sure to save a few "Snickerpoodles" from "Martha Jane's Bakery" for all good dogs who visit our classroom.

Our Invitation to Our Canine Friends ▶

Dear _____,

My class just finished reading <u>The Bookshop Dog</u> by Cynthia Rylant. The owner of the bookshop "loved her dog so much that she could hardly bear to be away from her. The woman took her dog to the park. She took her to the market. She even took her do to the dentist!" Just as Martha Jane, the bookshop dog, went everywhere with her owner, you are invited to school with your owners!

    If possible, please join us on _____ at _____. Please have a family member fill out the note below and return it to school with your young owner. Then, on the date above, have a family member drive you to school. Wear a leash, please. Your young owner will tell you about the school rules before you come to school. We look forward to your visit!

    Sincerely,

_____

Two Dogs and Two Cats: Graphing Activities

The back dust jacket of *The Bookshop Dog* shows a photo of Cynthia Rylant with her dog Martha Jane. The author description says Ms. Rylant lives in Oregon with her son, two cats, and two dogs. After sharing this information with students, we make a tabletop graph of "Our Pets."

    Prior to the lesson, label a sheet of construction paper with the names of possible pets—Dogs, Cats, Birds, Guinea Pigs, Hamsters, and Fish are some common pets to include. It may be a wise idea to allow space at the end of the graph for any pets you may have overlooked.

    Call on individual students to add one one Unifix cube to the graph for each of their pets. I add three cubes as well, one each for my two dogs and one cat. After all the markers have been added, discuss the results of your pet graph. Try comparing the total number of dogs to cats, fish to birds, the most popular pet and least popular pets, etc., then add all columns together for the total number of pets in your class.

Our Pet Graph
▼

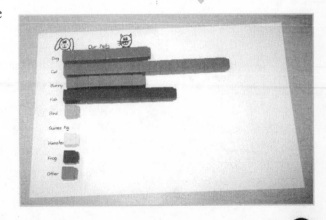

Love Your Pet: Making Posters to Encourage Responsible Pet Ownership

To Be a Responsible Pet Owner:

- LOVE your pet
- Groom your pet
- Feed and water your pet
- Take your pet to the vet regularly
- Care for your pet when he is sick
- Play with your pet
- Exercise your pet every day
- Take your pet to obedience school if needed

Martha Jane was well cared for by the big man in the green coat while the bookshop owner was in the hospital. He gave her a big yellow bow, made her smell like a flower garden, but most important, he had loved her. Begin a discussion of what it takes to be a responsible pet owner. List student ideas and have partners design posters to illustrate one of the ideas from the chart. Display the posters throughout the school or take to a local humane society to help others realize just what it takes to care for a pet.

More Books by Cynthia Rylant

All I See (Orchard Books, 1988)

Birthday Presents (Orchard Books, 1987)

Cat Heaven (Blue Sky Press, 1997)

The Cookie Store Cat (Blue Sky Press, 1999)

Dog Heaven (Blue Sky Press, 1995)

Henry and Mudge and the Bedtime Thumps (Macmillan Publishing Company, 1991)

Henry and Mudge in the Green Time (Bradbury Press, 1987)

Henry and Mudge Take the Big Test (Bradbury Press, 1991)

Henry and Mudge and the Wild Wind (Bradbury Press, 1993)

Night in the Country (Bradbury Press, 1986)

Poppleton Forever (Blue Sky Press, 1998)

Mr. Putter and Tabby Pour the Tea (Harcourt Brace & Company, 1994)

The Relatives Came (Simon & Schuster, 1985)

Scarecrow (Harcourt Brace & Company, 1998)

Silver Packages—An Appalachian Christmas Story (Orchard Books, 1987)

This Year's Garden (Bradbury Press, 1984)

Tulip Sees America (Blue Sky Press, 1998)

When I Was Young in the Mountains (E.P. Dutton, 1982)

Name _____ Date _____

Story Outline

Title: _____

Author: _____

Characters: _____

_____

Setting: _____

Beginning	Middle	Ending

Snickerpoodles

1 cup vegetable oil
1 cup shortening
2 cups honey
4 eggs
7 1/2 cups white flour
4 teaspoons cream of tartar
2 teaspoon baking soda
1 cup cornmeal
4 teaspoons cinnamon

Mix vegetable oil, shortening, and honey together until smooth. Add eggs and beat well. Blend in flour, baking soda, and cream of tartar. Knead dough until mixed well. Shape dough by rounded teaspoons into balls. Mix the cornmeal and the cinnamon together in a bowl and roll balls in mixture. Place 2 inches apart on a cookie sheet that has been sprayed with a nonstick spray. Press the balls down with a fork twice, going in two different directions. Bake 8 minutes at 400°. Remove from baking sheet and cool on a rack. Makes approximately 72 treats.

100 Skill-Building Lessons Using 10 Favorite Books   Scholastic Professional Books   Recipe from FOOD TV NETWORK, 1996